Creating a Language-Rich Math Class

What meanings do your students have for key mathematics concepts? What meanings do you wish them to have? *Creating a Language-Rich Math Class* offers practical approaches for developing conceptual understandings by connecting concrete, pictorial, verbal, and symbolic representations. The focus is on making mathematics memorable instead of on memorizing.

You'll learn strategies for introducing students to math language that gives meaning to the terms and symbols they use every day, for building flexibility and precision in students' use of math language, and for structuring activities to make them more language rich.

Book Features:

◆ Detailed directions for sample games and activities for immediate classroom use
◆ Investigations to Try and Questions for Reflection to assist in implementing these ideas into your practice
◆ Graphic organizer for helping students first understand, solve, and defend their solutions to word problems
◆ Blackline masters of game cards and puzzles (also available at www.routledge.com/9781138916296)

Sandra L. Atkins is committed to finding those "aha moments" when mathematical connections are made by teachers and students. She currently works with school districts across the United States through her company, Creating AHAs.

Other Eye On Education Books
Available from Routledge

(www.routledge.com/eyeoneducation)

Guided Math in Action:
Building Each Student's Mathematical Proficiency
with Small-Group Instruction
Nicki Newton

Math Workshop in Action:
Strategies for Grades K-5
Nicki Newton

Math Running Records in Action:
A Framework for Assessing Basic Fact Fluency in Grades K-5
Nicki Newton

Math Lesson Starters for the Common Core, Grades 6–8:
Activities Aligned to the Standards and Assessments
Paige Graiser

Less Is More in Elementary School:
Strategies for Thriving in a High-Stakes Environment
Renee Rubin, Michelle Abrego, and John Sutterby

The Mathematics Coaching Handbook:
Working with K-8 Teachers to Improve Instruction
Pia Hansen

A Collection of Performance Tasks and Rubrics:
Primary School Mathematics
Charlotte Danielson and Pia Hansen

A Collection of Performance Tasks and Rubrics:
Upper Elementary School Mathematics
Charlotte Danielson and Joshua Dragoon

A Collection of Performance Tasks and Rubrics:
Middle School Mathematics
Charlotte Danielson and Elizabeth Marquez

RtI in Math:
Evidence-Based Interventions for Struggling Students
Linda Forbringer and Wendy Fuchs

Creating a Language-Rich Math Class

Strategies and Activities for Building Conceptual Understanding

Sandra L. Atkins

Routledge
Taylor & Francis Group

NEW YORK AND LONDON

First published 2016
by Routledge
711 Third Avenue, New York, NY 10017

and by Routledge
2 Park Square, Milton Park, Abingdon, Oxon, OX14 4RN

Routledge is an imprint of the Taylor & Francis Group, an informa business

Library of Congress Cataloging-in-Publication Data
Atkins, Sandra L.
   Creating a language-rich math class : strategies and activities for
building conceptual understanding / by Sandra L. Atkins.
       pages cm
   Includes bibliographical references.
   1. Mathematics—Study and teaching (Early childhood)
2. Mathematics—Study and teaching (Elementary)   I. Title.
   QA135.6.A885 2016
   372.7—dc23
   2015013385

ISBN: 978-1-138-91628-9 (hbk)
ISBN: 978-1-138-91629-6 (pbk)
ISBN: 978-1-315-68975-3 (ebk)

Typeset in Palatino
by Apex CoVantage, LLC

Printed and bound in the United States of America by Publishers Graphics,
LLC on sustainably sourced paper.

Dedicated to

The teachers, principal, and that special third-grade class at
Crellin Elementary School

Contents

eResources. x
About the Author xi
Acknowledgments. xii
Introduction: Language? It's Mathematics!. xiv

**1 What Are They Really Thinking? Determining
the Meaning Kids Have for Terms** 1

2 Investigating Symbolic Decoding vs. Conceptual Language 7

3 Understanding the Meaning of the Operations 13
  Division. 14
      Partitive Division (Partitioning) 15
      Quotitive Division (Quotitioning) 16
  Multiplication. 18
      Equal Grouping Model 18
      Array Model 20
      Area Model 21
      Scaling. 24
  Subtraction 24
      Removal 24
      Comparison 25
      Difference as Distance 26
  Addition 28
      Joining. 28
      Part-Part-Total 29

4 Tips for Creating a Language-Rich Math Class 31
  Consider Sitting Down 32
  Are You Sure? How Did You Get Your Answer? 32
  Don't Be the Answer Key. 33
  Ask a Question to Help Them Change Their Minds 33
  Think, Pair, Share—Tell Me What Your Partner Said. 34

Have Students Use Four Representations (Concrete, Pictorial,
Verbal, Symbolic) Whenever Possible 35
Conceptual Language vs. Symbolic Decoding 36
Building and Using Language. 36

5   **Purposefully Choose and Use Materials** 39
Subitizing 39
Ten-Frame Domino Match. 41
Increasing the Cognitive Demand of the Experience. 43
Combinations for Ten 44
Using Materials to Build Conceptual Understandings 54

6   **Changing the Order for Introducing Mathematical
Language: Experience Then Name** 61
Experience First—A Look at Symmetry. 61
Area Investigations 65

7   **Structuring Activities to Make Them Language Rich**. 71
Tangram Communication Activity 72
Memory- or Concentration-Type Activities. 74

8   **Building Precision and Flexibility in Using
Mathematical Language** 79

9   **Making Sense of Word Problems: Developing
Independent Problem Solvers** 85
Beware of Key Words 85
Building Independent Problem Solvers. 86
Problem Solving Graphic Organizer 88
The Word Problem Solving Process 89
Sample Problem 1—Introducing the Process 90
Sample Problem 2—Debriefing Problems 92
Sample Problem 3—Don't Let Your Past Interfere With
the Students' Problem Solving 95

Conclusion: Give Students the Gift of Time. 99

Blackline Masters 103
Ten-Frame Dominos 104
Sample Concentration Game Cards 107

Tangram Piece Master 110
Sample Tangram Puzzles 111
Sample "I Have . . . Who Has?" Cards 113
Word Problem Graphic Organizer 116
Sample Word Problems 117

eResources

The Blackline Masters from the book are also available on our website so you can print and use them in your own classroom. The material includes the following:

- Ten-Frame Dominos
- Sample Concentration Game Cards
- Tangram Piece Master
- Sample Tangram Puzzles
- Sample "I Have . . . Who Has?" Cards
- Word Problem Graphic Organizer
- Sample Word Problems

To download those items, go to the book product page, www.routledge.com/9781138916296. Then click on the tab that says "eResources," and select the files. They will begin downloading to your computer.

About the Author

Dr. Sandy Atkins is the owner and executive director of Creating AHAs, LLC. An inspiring speaker, Dr. Atkins is committed to finding those "aha moments" when mathematical connections are made by teachers and students. Her sessions are thought-provoking and practical.

Sandy is passionate about helping *all* students understand mathematics. With particular interest in effective mathematics intervention, Sandy works closely with teachers across the United States to help them pinpoint student disconnects and close mathematical concept gaps. Dr. Atkins enjoys opportunities to provide keynote talks, workshops, seminars, and presentations. But her favorite professional development activities involve building relationships with teachers through ongoing site-based projects that include getting into classrooms and learning from students. Sandy loves hearing, "Oh I get it! Why wasn't I taught this way?" AHA!

Dr. Atkins is also the author of *Creating Fraction and Decimal AHAs*, a resource that provides a systematic approach for helping students understand and even enjoy learning about fractions and decimals.

Please contact Sandy Atkins, Ph.D., at Creating AHAs for additional information.
www.creatingahas.com
Email: info@creatingahas.com

Acknowledgments

There are many people who have influenced my thinking about teaching and learning as described in the pages of this book . . . mathematics just happens to be the focus. First there were my teachers: Tom Denmark, Grayson Wheatley, Elizabeth Jakubowski, and Catherine Emihovich. Fellow students: Anne Reynolds, Sandy Trowell, Tad Watanabe, and Ricardo Dreyfous. My students: Drs. Lynn Cowen, Jill Perry, Dana McCauley, and Dave Kennedy. All who challenged my thinking when I thought I had it all figured out.

Then there were my colleagues Calvin and Rosemary Irons, Honi Bamberger, and James Burnett who helped me understand how to make mathematics fun and accessible to students. I can't forget all of the teachers and students who have invited me into their classrooms and shared their thinking with me . . . and who challenged my thinking when I thought I had it all figured out.

Finally, there are those individuals who may not know they were my teachers. Some taught me as I watched them present or work with children: Carole Greenes, Carol Findell, Juanita Copley, Mari Muri, Ruth Parker, Marilyn Burns, Kathy Richardson, Jo Boaler, and Jodean Grunow. Others whose books and articles made my head hurt . . . in a good way: Eleanor Duckworth, Constance Kamii, Susan Ohanian, Vivian Paley, Phyllis and David Whitin, Gary Tsuruda, Rebecca Corwin, Donna Williams, Oliver Sacks, and so many others.

All of these names are people who helped me grow in my thinking over the past 30 years . . . especially when I thought I had it all figured out.

Thank you!

I can't forget the names of people in my present. Family, friends, and colleagues who graciously read and commented on various generations of the book: Sue Atkins, Amy Howell, Kathy Taylor, Becky Sanders, and Dana McCauley. I can't thank you enough for your insights, feedback, words of encouragement, and keeping me on schedule in spite of my procrastination and tight deadlines. Then there are the editors, designers, and all of those talented individuals at Routledge and Apex CoVantage that have helped breathe life into this book: Lauren Davis, Marlena Sullivan, Marie Roberts, and many others. Thank you for your patience, encouragement, and guidance throughout this process.

Thank you!

Last but not least, thank you for reading this long acknowledgment. As you read through the chapters of this book may your head hurt . . . in a good way.

Introduction

Language? It's Mathematics!

I was going to visit a friend who had just moved to Pittsburgh. She had emailed directions to her new house. About a third of the way through it said, "Continue down the windy road for about a mile." Now when you read that I bet you thought of a road with a lot of curves. Not me. I'll claim that I was tired. When I read it I wondered how she knew there would be wind on the road that day . . . as in gusts of . . . wind tunnel. Not one of my finer moments. It did make me laugh at the time. It still makes me smile and shake my head.

Language is tricky. Think about bough, dough, rough, and tough. What about "read" being either past or present tense depending on the pronunciation? I could go on but you get my point. Mathematical words are also tricky. A single word can have multiple meanings depending on context. A "second" is a unit of time but it is also a position in line. Some words have everyday meanings and we give them mathematics-specific meanings. "Similar" is just one example. Its everyday meaning describes things that are almost alike but not exactly alike. In mathematics it means proportional. Then there are mathematics-specific words such as minus or subtract and words that describe the materials we use. Whew!

The sad thing is that many people do not think of mathematics as being language rich, but it is. We cannot discuss mathematics without using words. Story problems require an ability to read and comprehend language, especially language used in math contexts. Context helps us know if "windy" is a curvy road or if it's a great day to fly a kite. Constructing viable arguments and critiquing the reasoning of others is quite challenging without language. Most importantly, language provides us with a window into the understandings children have about key mathematical concepts.

A language-rich mathematics class is an exciting place. Students are describing their thinking, defending their answers, and discussing mathematical ideas. Children who struggle with memorizing facts and procedures have a way to make sense of mathematics. They are able to connect mathematical symbols to things they can touch, things they can draw, and language. Learning mathematics shifts from memorizing to engaging in activities that are memorable.

What are we doing? We're finding out what our students think, purposefully designing tasks, using conceptual language, and encouraging students to talk with one another. What is the most important thing we'll do to create a language-rich mathematics class? Learn to be quiet and listen. After all, who needs the most practice talking?

I'll warn you though. It may not all be smooth sailing. I had been asked to do a lesson in a first-grade classroom. I decided to do something on fractions. I wanted the children to understand that if I divided a whole into two pieces, they both needed to be the same size to be called halves. We were seated in a circle on the floor. I had drawn a large circle on a large sheet of paper. I cut it into two pieces but the pieces weren't the same size. I labeled each piece "½."

I placed the drawing in the center of our circle and asked the children what they thought. Nobody said anything. I asked, "If this were a cake and I cut it this way, what would you think?" Silence. I took scissors and cut the "cake" into the two pieces. I gave the large piece to one student and the small piece to another. I again asked, "If this were cake or pie, what would you think?" Nothing. I took the pieces back and cut them again into uneven pieces. Distributed the pieces and asked my question again. They just sat quietly, waiting patiently.

Now this was supposed to be a language-rich lesson, the focus of this book. But they weren't saying anything. There were other teachers watching and I was getting nowhere. I'm sure you can predict how I was feeling. I stuck with it though. I took back pieces and several more times cut the "cake" into smaller pieces and gave the pieces to children who didn't have a "slice" yet. Each time I asked what they thought. Same reaction. Polite silence. Finally every child had a piece of this "cake." Some had nice large pieces and some very small pitiful slices. I asked one last time.

Finally the first little girl I had given the large "half" to raised her hand. I was hopeful. I asked again. She looked at me and said, "Mrs. Hughes says it is better to have something than nothing and you should be happy you have anything at all."

Are you kidding me? I turned and looked at Mrs. Hughes and the other teachers and they just started laughing. No wonder I couldn't get them to discuss the fairness of the size of the pieces. Mrs. Hughes had done a wonderful job of getting children to stop bickering when they might not have the exact amount as their neighbor. They were being extremely polite for their guest teacher. It sure did affect what I thought was going to be a great language-rich discussion.

Throughout the book we'll examine techniques for building conceptual understanding and creating a language-rich mathematics class. As you'll see, it takes time to develop mathematical language. It requires us to sit down, be quiet, be curious, and listen to what the children are saying. Don't be surprised if some of your other "class lessons" creep into your math conversations . . . "happy to have anything at all." Really! One of the teachers tried a similar lesson with her class. After the first cut, she asked a student which piece she would like. The student selected the smaller piece and said that she was trying to watch her fat content. They had just finished a nutrition unit.

As you try the activities for creating a language-rich mathematics class described in this book, remember to give children many opportunities to test out the language of mathematics. Let them share what they think and allow them to make missteps. If we listen carefully to what they say instead of what we hope to hear, we will learn about their mathematical understandings. Sometimes we may even smile. We may smile because of their sophistication in explaining their thinking. We may smile at their creativity in solving problems and making us think. We might even smile at the "windy-windy" confusion they have or laugh aloud as they foil a great launch to a mathematically language-rich discussion. After all, it is better to have something than nothing.

In each chapter I've included *Investigations to Try* and *Questions for Reflection*. I hope you will try these investigations and reflect on the questions. I also hope this is not an independent journey. Talk with your peers about your thinking, your questions, your wonderings, and your AHAs. As I hope you'll see, a language-rich experience is very powerful for us all.

Question for Reflection

What stories came to mind regarding your students' struggles with language, in particular mathematical language?

1

What Are They Really Thinking?

Determining the Meaning
Kids Have for Terms

Many years ago I spoke with several kindergarten students about time. I asked Jonathan what time words he knew. Jonathan said, "Seconds." I said, "Seconds? What's a second?" He held up two fingers and said, "twos." I thought he was thinking of seconds as two things or perhaps a place in line, second. Luckily I stayed quiet and he continued. "You get some and then get some more." I admit that I still wasn't sure about what Jonathan meant until he said, "foods." Oh! It then hit me . . . Helpings! This kindergartner knew that seconds was a time word but his meaning for it was what happened at mealtime. Wow!

We know students struggle with terminology. Sometimes we are so focused on making sure that students have the "correct" meaning for terms that we miss opportunities to learn what they are really thinking. We end up trying to fix a problem before we know what the problem is. Our fix is often providing a definition and some additional examples. However, Jonathan's meaning for seconds made sense based on his experiences. I was actually surprised when he picked seconds. He may have just heard an adult say, "Give me a second" or "Wait a second." I don't really know why Jonathan thought that seconds was a time word; I should have asked him. But based on what we do know, we can use a more targeted approach for refining or expanding Jonathan's current understanding. What would you do?

During that same week I spoke with two first-grade girls, Elise and Celia. I asked each girl the same three questions:

- ◆ How long are you at P.E.?
- ◆ How long are you at school?
- ◆ How long do you sleep at night?

I first interviewed Elise.

S: How long are you at P.E.?
E: Six minutes.
S: How long are you at school?
E: About ten minutes.
S: How long do you sleep at night?
E: About an hour.

I should mention that this interview occurred in May. I was thinking we had a little work to do with Elise. I then interviewed Celia.

S: How long are you at P.E.?
C: We go at 9:30. I'd say twenty or thirty minutes.
S: How long are you at school?
C: Six or seven hours.

It is not surprising to see this dramatic difference in understanding in first grade. Celia was in the ballpark on both counts. I was thinking, "Wow, Celia has a pretty good understanding of duration for a first-grader." I then asked her the next question.

S: How long do you sleep at night?
C: I do this sometimes. I know there's twenty-four hours in a day but I don't know yet how long night is.

Take a moment to think about that. Do all of your students know that twenty-four hours includes night and day?

I gathered my wits about me and continued.

S: So when you think of day, what do you think of?
C: You know. When it's light out. I think night is a little shorter. I think it's like twenty-one hours.

Wow!

As we saw with Jonathan and now with Celia, our everyday language sometimes interferes with the mathematical meanings for terms. Seconds is something you get at mealtime. Second is also a position and it is a length of time. Day is when it is light out, daytime and daylight, but it is also a unit of time. How do we help students sort out these meanings? It isn't so easy, is it?

After the interview I spoke with Celia's teacher, Ron. I told him that Celia did not understand that the twenty-four hours in a day included daytime and nighttime. Ron was great at using puppets and literature within his math lessons. He developed a week of lessons on time. He read books about time. His puppets talked about time. He showed a circle, half of which he had colored yellow and the other half midnight blue. He wanted to show that the twenty-four hours included night and day. He even asked Celia if she was with him when talking about the twenty-four hours including both. She said, "Yeah, yeah."

At the end of the week I spoke with Celia again.

S: What did you learn about time?
C: I learned there's twenty-four hours in a day.
S: Does that include night?
C: Nah. I still haven't figured that out yet.

Have I said, "WOW!"?

I observed the lessons that Ron did to help his students make sense of time. They were great. But at the end of that week Celia said, "I still haven't figured that out yet." Understanding mathematics, communicating mathematically, and learning mathematical language takes time. It requires us to take time to find out the meanings students have for terms and concepts. We may need to throw a wrench in their thinking by giving a counter-example or providing experiences that will expand their understandings to other contexts.

I have had many two-by-four experiences throughout my career. These experiences, similar to being hit upside the head, got my attention and made me think about the ways in which I was assessing student understanding. How often were my assessments misleading? If I had asked Celia, "How many hours in a day?," she would have confidently said, "twenty-four." I would have checked off that objective as complete without realizing that Celia did not know that night was included in the twenty-four hours. That's a pretty big gap to go unnoticed.

Years ago Art Linkletter had a variety show with a segment called "Kids Say the Darndest Things." (You can find clips on YouTube.) During the show the host would masterfully interview children to entertain viewers. The children always got big laughs because, "they were so cute!" What they said would often embarrass their parents. But it also revealed what they really thought. The audience, often to the parents' horror, heard the meaning the children were giving to unfamiliar words and phrases, or perhaps familiar but misunderstood words and phrases. The host didn't correct the kids. He actually asked additional questions to see what more he could learn. For our mathematical purposes we aren't trying to entertain audiences, but we are trying to get to the bottom of what kids are thinking.

Interviewing children is a powerful tool for determining their conceptual understandings (Huinker, 1993). It allows us to find out what students are really thinking so we can provide targeted experiences that can throw a wrench in their thinking, expand their thinking, or introduce them to new concepts. What we learn helps us make informed instructional decisions. But we need to remember that the interview is not the time for teaching. It is a time for learning. Once you find a misconception, don't stop and fix it immediately, pursue it. Ask additional questions. Try to determine if there are other related misunderstandings. And take great notes.

Interview Guidelines
1.   Be a learner. You are trying to understand the meaning students have for terms.
2.   Be curious.
3.   Be quiet. If they don't answer right away that's okay. Give them time to think.
4.   Put on your curious or interested face. Let them think this is a time for them to teach you a thing or two.
5.   Once you find a misconception ask follow-up questions to learn more about what students are thinking and why.
6.   Save your desire to fix a misconception for later. The interview is a time to learn what your students are thinking.

Now, if you're thinking that's just what happens with young children, I hope you'll think again. A colleague of mine showed me a paper that one of her fourth-graders had turned in. It was a vocabulary quiz. The students were verbally given several data analysis terms. They were to define by using words or pictures. This student had drawn pictures for each of his answers. For "mean" he drew a mean face, for "mode", a picture of a lawn mower. For "range" he drew a shooting range. For "median" he drew a picture of that place in the center of a highway. Like Celia and Jonathan, he had everyday meanings for the terms but not mathematical meanings.

Although we hope there is no confusion about mathematical terms as students progress through each grade, there is. While interviewing two middle school girls regarding ratio and proportion concepts I asked them what similar means. They pulled two chapter books off the shelf and eloquently explained to me the ways in which they were similar. It was great. But in mathematics similarity represents proportionality. Think of shrinking or enlarging a shape. Again, these students had everyday meanings for terms but not mathematical meanings.

I admit that I love finding these misconceptions. If a lesson reveals all the misunderstandings that students have, it has been a great day. For some of those teachers whose classes I'm in . . . not so much. They are often mortified to find that the students didn't understand all they thought they did after working so hard to teach them the material. For me, we have uncovered what we need to do next.

To help students build conceptual understandings and create a language-rich mathematics class, we must first determine the meanings students have for concepts and terms. It involves listening and understanding what they say versus listening and leading them to what we hope to hear (Corwin, 1996; Paley, 1996). Sometimes this requires coming in through the back door; that is, asking a student about night instead of day. Until we determine what the problem is we have little hope of fixing it.

Questions for Reflection and Investigations to Try

1. What experiences would help Jonathan increase his understanding of multiple meaning words such as "seconds"?
2. What experiences would help Celia understand that twenty-four hours includes "day" and "night"?
3. What other mathematical terms have everyday meanings?
4. What questions could you ask your students that would determine their understandings of key concepts and terms? Remember to listen to what they say versus leading them to say what you hope to hear.
5. Over the next few days try to determine the meaning your students have for key mathematical concepts and terms. Record anecdotes of their understandings.

References

Corwin, R.B. (1996). *Talking Mathematics*. Portsmouth, NH: Heinemann.

Huinker, D. (1993). Interviews: A Window to Students' Conceptual Knowledge of the Operations. In N.L. Webb & A.F. Coxford (Eds.), *Assessment in Mathematics Classrooms* (pp. 80–86). Reston, VA: The National Council of Teachers of Mathematics, Inc.

Paley, V.G. (1996). On Listening to What the Children Say. In R.B. Corwin, J. Storeygard, & S.L. Price (Eds.), *Talking Mathematics* (pp. 113–127). Portsmouth, NH: Heinemann.

2

Investigating Symbolic Decoding vs. Conceptual Language

Have you ever caught yourself thinking for your students? A student says something and you immediately write it down, thinking you know what they are meaning? Or do you interpret the symbols for your students? I know I have engaged in both practices.

A two-by-four moment hit me when I was interviewing a third-grade student. As we were talking I became concerned about his subtraction under-standings. I finally wrote "5 – 3" on the board. Without reading it to him I asked him, "How do you solve this?" He told me that you have to cross out the three and give some to the five. Uh oh! He was trying to regroup. They must have been spending a lot of time practicing the regrouping algorithm.

There happened to be some cubes on the table. I asked him to show me five cubes. He did. I asked him to take away three cubes. He did. I asked how many were left. Without hesitation he said, "Two." I then pointed to the "5 – 3" written on the board and again asked him how you solve it. He said that you have to cross out the three . . . . That got my attention! He wasn't connecting "5 – 3" to what he had just modeled with the cubes. Who was primarily inter-preting the symbols? I was. Was I writing the symbolic notation for what I thought the students meant? You betcha! When I did have the students read the symbols, what was I expecting to hear? I was listening for what I was hoping to hear, which was the way I would read the symbols. How was I reading the symbols? I was definitely symbol-naming.

Suppose I have an opportunity to visit your classroom. I walk up to the board and without saying anything I write, "3 + 7." I then ask the students to write in words how they would read the expression. What would your students write? What would you write? Teachers I work with say, "three plus seven." When asked what percentage of the time their students would read the expression as three plus seven, they say 100%. But consider this. What percentage of time is the word "plus" in a word problem?

Let's face it. As soon as students are introduced to the operation symbols (+, −, ×, ÷) their language becomes primarily symbolic. "3 + 7" is read as three plus seven, "7 − 3" as seven minus three, "3 × 7" as three times seven, and "7 ÷ 3" as seven divided by three. Students are naming the symbols (symbolic decoding). When I ask this same group of teachers what their students struggle with in mathematics, I guarantee that "word problems" will be on the list. Multi-step word problems will get special recognition. To determine the specific disconnect I ask, "What do your students struggle with when solving word problems?" Would you be surprised to hear, "Choosing the appropriate operation"? I'm not. Is it really a surprise when the students' primary understanding of the symbol is its name?

Let's go back to your classroom. Your students have recorded their "word" translation for "3 + 7." As predicted, most, if not all, have written, "three plus seven." I then say, "Write how you could read this a different way. A third way." As we look out over your class don't be surprised if your students are looking at me like I have a horn growing out of my head. It happens. Giving them time to think, to realize that I'm serious and that you won't help them, some students will write "seven plus three." Others will write "three add seven."

Table 2.1

+	plus, add
−	minus, subtract
×	times, multiply
÷	divided by

For our purposes, symbolic decoding is the symbol naming described above.

As we've all experienced, students who are proficient at symbolic decoding are not necessarily mathematically proficient. Symbolic decoding does not correlate with understanding symbol meaning.

Symbolic decoding is not restricted to the operations. I recently interviewed a group of fifth- and sixth-grade students. One fifth-grader read "11.7" as "one, one, point seven." I admit I wasn't expecting that. I was expecting her next answer. When asked if she could read it a different way she said, "eleven point seven." So did all of the other fifth- and sixth-grade students.

We've all heard this. Maybe we've even read 11.7 in this way. However, this symbol-by-symbol decoding, a common practice in many classrooms, does not develop an understanding of the numbers or place value, or connect to prior work with common fractions. Precisely reading 11.7 as eleven and seven-tenths develops all of these relationships.

Investigation to Try

Determine your students' translations for the operations. Write an expression such as,

$$3 + 7$$
$$7 - 3$$
$$4 \times 6$$

$$12 \div 3 \text{ or } 3\overline{\smash{)}12}$$

(I show both division expressions and ask students to translate.)

Then ask the following two questions. Both answers should be related to the chosen expression.

1. Without reading aloud, ask students to write in words how they would read the expression. Ask them to write it a different way. Then, perhaps, a third way.
2. Ask students to draw a picture.

Note: You may find that your students have done a symbol-by-symbol drawing. That is, their pictures also reflect symbolic decoding. Don't be surprised if you see:

$$\text{ooo} + \text{ooooooo}$$
$$\text{ooooooo} - \text{ooo}$$
$$\text{oooo} \times \text{oooooo}$$
$$\text{oooooooooooo} \div \text{ooo}$$

These also reflect the students' understandings, or perhaps lack of understanding, of the operations.

Questions for Reflection

1. Which expression did you use? How did your students translate the expression? What terms did they use to describe the operation?
2. What pictures did they draw? Were they symbol-by-symbol drawings? What did you learn about your students' understandings?
3. Examine the drawings of Student 1 and Student 2 in the table below. What are the differences in these students' understandings based on their illustrations?

Table 2.2

Problem	Student 1	Student 2
7 - 3	⊙⊙⊙⊙⊙⊙⊙ - ⊙⊙⊙	⊙⊙⊙⊙⊛⊛⊛
4 × 6	⊙⊙⊙⊙ × ⊙⊙⊙⊙⊙⊙	⊙⊙⊙⊙⊙⊙ ⊙⊙⊙⊙⊙⊙ ⊙⊙⊙⊙⊙⊙ ⊙⊙⊙⊙⊙⊙
12 ÷ 3	⊙⊙⊙⊙⊙⊙⊙⊙⊙⊙⊙⊙ ÷ ⊙⊙⊙	⊗⊗ ⊗⊗ ⊗⊗

To build conceptual understandings of the operations, students and teachers need to use conceptual language translations of symbolic representations. Instead of "three plus seven," we would translate as "three put together with seven," "three combined with seven," "three joined with seven," or perhaps "three and seven." Each of these translations connect the potential action of the operation to the mathematical symbol "+." It assists students in understanding the meaning of the operation (Carpenter et al., 1999).

I'm not saying that students should not know symbolic names. They should. But we need to dramatically decrease the amount of time that we use symbolic decoding and dramatically increase the use of conceptual language translations. What if about 10% of the time 3 + 7 was read as three plus seven and about 90% of the time a conceptual language translation was used: three put together with seven, three joined with seven, three combined with seven?

Table 2.3

Symbol	Symbolic Decoding	Conceptual Language
+	plus, add, sum	put together, join, combine
−	minus, subtract, difference	remove, take away, how many fewer, how many more, difference (distance concept)
×	times, multiply, product	groups of, rows of, jumps of, rectangle ___ by ___ (2 factors)
÷	divided by, quotient	separated into equal groups of, rows of, jumps of, lengths of (partitive division) How many ___ are in ___? (quotitive or measurement division)

When students are solving problems involving putting things together they would connect it to addition. When combining equal groups they would think . . . multiplication.

A lack of conceptual language fluency can impact the understanding of algebraic expressions, equations, and inequalities that students are asked to solve as they progress in mathematics. A simple equation such as $x + 2 = 5$ has traditionally been solved using a series of symbolic manipulations. However, students know that three put together with two is five or that two more than three is five. Instead of decoding as "x plus two equals five," read as "two more than what number is five?" or "two combined with what number is five?" Solving this simple equation then focuses on determining the unknown. Likewise, $2x - 3 = 7$ could be translated as "three fewer than what double is seven?" Again, students can reason about these numeric relationships to determine the value of x, understanding that a single solution is needed. If three fewer than a double is seven, we know that the double must be ten. What double is ten? Five. So x must be five.

As algebraic representations become more complex, conceptual language translations are even more important. Consider $xy > 0$. It doesn't look very nice. We expect students to know that when an operation symbol is absent we are multiplying. In the case of $xy > 0$, students would typically decode the symbols as "xy greater than zero." Because students spend a lot of time practicing techniques for solving for y, many students use that strategy to solve $xy > 0$. They try to divide both sides by x. This strategy does not work in this case. But what if conceptual language versus symbolic naming were used to read $xy > 0$? That is, what if we read $xy > 0$ as, "When is the product of two numbers positive?" This translation provides access to the mathematics that symbolic decoding does not. This is now a problem that requires an understanding of the effect on multiplication when working with positive and negative numbers. The product will be positive if both numbers are positive or both numbers are negative. This means that any ordered pair in Quadrants I or III on the coordinate plane (not including the axes) would be a solution to this inequality.

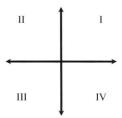

Shifting our focus from symbolic decoding to conceptual language translations builds an understanding of the operations, number, equality, and inequality in all we do in mathematics. In this way, we are building the language of word problems as students learn computation strategies, build number sense, and solve simple algebraic equations. We are also giving students access to doing mathematics because they understand the meaning of the symbols. Comprehending the symbols versus decoding them develops a depth of understanding of mathematics.

Questions for Reflection

1. I mentioned the importance of reading decimal numbers such as 11.7 as "eleven and seven-tenths" instead of "one, one, point seven" or "eleven point seven." What are some other examples of symbolic decoding (e.g., ⅔ as two over three)?
2. In which contexts would a symbol-by-symbol naming be appropriate (e.g., phone numbers)?
3. What strategies will you use to increase the use of conceptual language translations in your classroom?

Reference

Carpenter, T. P., Fennema, E., Franke, M. L., Levi, L., & Empson, S. B. (1999). *Children's Mathematics. Cognitively Guided Instruction.* Portsmouth, NH: Heinemann.

3

Understanding the Meaning
of the Operations

When I was learning to compute, focus was given to mastering arithmetic algorithms (step-by-step procedures). We would learn the algorithms for addition without regrouping, then addition with regrouping; subtraction without regrouping, then subtraction with regrouping; and so on. The focus was on mastering specific answer-getting techniques (Daro, 2014). Although I did master my facts and those algorithms, I still struggled with solving word problems and other non-routine problems. I had mastered the procedures, algorithmic fluency, without understanding the meanings of the operations. As a result, it was difficult for me to choose the appropriate operation or represent problems mathematically when trying to solve word problems. Would this be true for any of your students?

In the past, algorithmic fluency was the focus of much of the elementary curriculum. With the evolution of Standards documents (National Council of Teachers of Mathematics, 1989, 2000; National Governors Association Center for Best Practices & Council of Chief State School Officers, 2010), computation strategies have become the focus. We hope that students become fluent with a variety of mental computation strategies so that paper and pencil becomes their last choice, not their first. For example, students might think of $199 + 199$ as double two hundred minus two, $200 + 200 - 2$ (a near double). Other students might think of $199 + 199$ as $200 + 198$. They are bridging to ten or 100. These are both very efficient strategies for which paper and pencil is not needed.

In some cases, strategies are becoming the new algorithms. They are becoming the new answer-getting techniques. What if we shift our focus to first understanding the meaning of the operations? The models for the operations help us understand possible problem contexts, potential pictorial representations, and related conceptual language translations.

As we saw with symbolic decoding, students who can fluently solve computation problems may not be as successful at solving word problems or generalizing relationships as we ask them to reason algebraically. In this chapter we will delve deeper into the models for the operations and their meanings (Carpenter et al., 1999; Chapin & Johnson, 2006). The goal is for students to work flexibly with a variety of these models when computing. This will shift to understanding how they are to operate on the numbers instead of recalling the steps of memorized algorithms. It will also build a language-symbol connection that will assist students in understanding word problem contexts and generalizing relationships as we ask them to reason algebraically. As we examine the models for the operations, consider your students' current understandings and flexibility in using each of the models. What are their understandings versus their computational skills?

Instead of starting with addition and then moving to subtraction, multiplication, and division, let's do the reverse. Let's begin our discussion with division, then move to multiplication, subtraction, and end with addition. Please don't think I'm suggesting that you switch your scope and sequence. If you teach in the primary grades, you may be thinking that you can skip the sections on division and multiplication. I hope you'll read on. Division and multiplication contexts are meaningful to young children.

Division

A kindergarten class went on a field trip to a local farm. To continue with the farming theme, the next day the teacher, Lesa, gathered the children together in a circle on the floor. Lesa had a sack of potatoes. There happened to be twenty potatoes in the sack. Lesa told the children that Farmer Joe had four neighbors to whom he'd like to give the potatoes. He wanted to make sure it was fair and wondered if the class would help make sure each neighbor got the same amount. Lesa put four plates out, one for each neighbor. The children understood the problem. They counted the potatoes and found there were twenty. They then decided that they could put one potato on each plate until they used them all up. They partitioned the sack of potatoes into four equal groups.

Now, the story doesn't end there. If you know anything about potatoes, you know they aren't a uniform size. When I looked at the plates there were both large and small potatoes. I pulled two of the plates toward me and told the children I was standing at the fence talking with my neighbor when Farmer Joe brings us each a plate of potatoes. I told the children to watch carefully. I said, "Hocus pocus" as I put the five largest potatoes on one of the plates and the five smallest potatoes on the other. We counted the potatoes on each plate to make sure there were still five. I continued by telling the children that Farmer Joe gave my neighbor the plate with the five large potatoes and me the plate with the five small potatoes. I said that I didn't think that was fair and square (a term that Lesa always used) and asked what we could do to make it fair. We talked a bit and then I left.

When I returned later that day Lesa had a couple of the children share their solution. They showed me three photos. The first photo they said was their first solution. The second was when I said, "Hocus pocus." It showed five large potatoes on one plate and five small potatoes on the other. The third was what they did to make it fair and square. I looked at the photo to see that they had cut the potatoes to make them about the same size. I noticed there were now more than five potatoes on a plate. I asked why the number had changed from five. The children explained that each neighbor got the same number and the same size. As you can see, young children can begin to explore the concept of separating a set into equal groups, partition, to make the groups "fair and square."

Partitive Division (Partitioning)

Partitive division or partitioning (Carpenter et al., 1999; Otto et al., 2011) involves knowing the total (whole), knowing the number of groups (parts), and finding the number (amount) in each group. If we think of $12 \div 2$ in terms of partitioning or partitive division, we know there is a total of twelve that we are to separate into two equal groups.

Twelve separated into two equal groups is six per group.

What if we were to think of $1 \div 5$ in terms of partitioning? We have a whole that we are to separate (partition) into five equal parts.

When done, each part will be one-fifth of the whole.

This type of division also holds for a fraction divided by a whole number such as 1½ ÷ 2. We are separating (partitioning) one and a half into two equal parts or groups.

$$1\frac{1}{2} \div 2$$

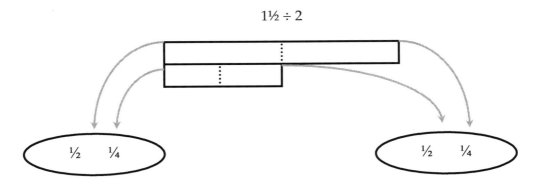

We can separate the whole into two halves and place a half in each group. Likewise, we can separate the half into two one-fourth pieces, and place a fourth in each group. We then combine the half and fourth pieces to get three-fourths. Therefore, one and a half separated into two equal groups, or parts, is three-fourths.

Notice that in each case we translated "÷" as "separated into." This model for division provides us with one of the conceptual language translations for division, "_____ separated into _____ equal groups (or parts)."

Table 3.1

Operation	Model	Conceptual Language
Division	Partitive Division or Partitioning	_____ separated into _____ equal groups

Quotitive Division (Quotitioning)

When I think of partitive division I think of the scenarios in Pat Hutchins' *The Doorbell Rang* (1986). In the story there is a plate of cookies being shared among a given number of children. Another division scenario involves knowing the number needed in a group. For this scenario I think of filling egg cartons. I know that a dozen eggs fit in each carton. If I'm starting with forty-eight eggs, I know I can fill four cartons as I "pull out" or measure off groups of twelve. This type of division is referred to as quotitive division.

Quotitive division or quotitioning involves knowing the total (whole), knowing the number (amount) in each group, and finding the number of groups (parts). I also think of this as measurement division (Carpenter et al., 1999; Otto et al., 2011). Perhaps you'll see why with some examples. Let's revisit 12 ÷ 2 in terms of quotitioning or quotitive division. We know there are a total of twelve and that we are to pull out or measure off groups of two. We are to find how many groups of two we will be able to make with a quantity of twelve.

In this case there are six groups of two in twelve.

The associated conceptual language translation for quotitive division is, "How many _____ in _____?" For our problem, 12 ÷ 2, we would translate as, "How many twos are in twelve?"

This model is very helpful when thinking about fraction division. Using a quotitive division translation, we would read 1½ ÷ ¼ as, "How many fourths are in one and a half?" We know there are four in the whole and two more in the half, so there are six.

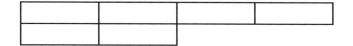

Using the above rectangular model to represent 1½ ÷ ¼, we see that we essentially measured off the number of fourths that would fit into one and a half.

Table 3.2

Operation	Model	Conceptual Language
Division	Partitive Division or Partitioning	_____ separated into _____ equal groups
	Quotitive Division or Quotitioning (Measurement)	How many _____ are in _____?

I hope you see that students need to understand and use both models for division. It does not make sense to translate 1½ ÷ ¼ as "one and a half separated into one-fourth equal groups." Likewise, we would not translate 1½ ÷ 2 as "How many twos are in one and a half?" However, using the appropriate conceptual language translation helps me think about the action that is taking place. For 1½ ÷ ¼ I'm trying to find the number of fourths in one and a half whereas for 1½ ÷ 2, I'm trying to separate one and a half into two equal groups or parts. These actions of separating or measuring off are similar to the actions students will see in context problems or word problems.

Multiplication

As with division, there are several models for multiplication (Carpenter et al., 1999; Otto et al., 2011). Since multiplication and division are inverse operations, if one model for division is separating into equal groups, then one model for multiplication is combining equal groups.

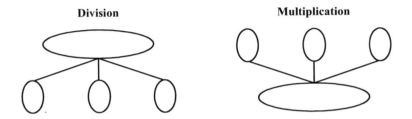

Equal Grouping Model

Repeated addition is often used to introduce students to multiplication. In the early grades, multiplication is introduced as a specialized form of addition. As with addition, we join or combine groups or distances. However, with multiplication, they must be equal groups or equal distances.

Let's revisit that same kindergarten class. One day the students were helping Lesa decide how many apples she would need for her daughter's lunch for the school week. Lesa gave her daughter two apples each day — one for lunch and one for snack. The children had five paper bags and used cubes as apples to put into each bag. Five groups of two means Lesa needed ten apples.

If we think of 3 × 4 using an equal grouping model, we would have three groups of four.

What about 3 × 14, three groups of fourteen? Instead of drawing fourteen dots in each group, let's use a more efficient tool. Let's replace the dots with base ten materials.

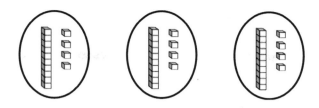

In this case we think of fourteen as ten and four, 14 = 10 + 4. As a result we have three groups of fourteen represented as three groups of ten put together with three groups of four.

$$3 \times 14 = 3(10+14)$$
$$= 3 \times 10 + 3 \times 4$$

As you can see, the equal grouping model is great for introducing students to the Distributive Property. Although the symbolic representation looks complicated, the conceptual language translations are very accessible to young students.

Three groups of fourteen is the same as three groups of ten put together with three groups of four.

The beauty of the Distributive Property is that it is not restricted to whole number multiplication. The equal grouping model can be used to represent the multiplication of whole numbers and mixed numbers (e.g., 3 × 2½) or whole numbers and fractions less than one (e.g., 3 × ½). Consider 3×2½, three groups of two and a half.

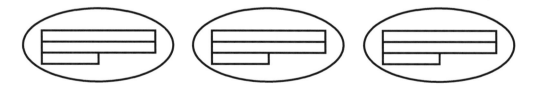

For this representation we think of two and a half as two wholes put together with one half,

$$2½ = 2 + ½$$

To represent three groups of two and a half, 3 × 2½, we use three groups of two put together with three groups of one-half, 3 × 2 + 3 × 2½.

$$3 \times 2½ = 3(2 + ½)$$
$$= 3 \times 2 + 3 \times ½$$

The equal grouping model can be used to represent equal quantities as well as equal distances. In the early grades these are often described as equal jumps on a number line.

In each of the above examples we translated multiplication as equal groups or equal jumps of ____. This provides one of our conceptual language translations for multiplication.

Table 3.3

Operation	Model	Conceptual Language
Multiplication	Equal Groups; Equal Distances	____ groups of _____ "jumps" of ____

Array Model

We can also visually represent multiplication using an array model. Elinor J. Pinczes' *One Hundred Hungry Ants* (1993) provides wonderful illustrations of the array model. With this model, multiplication is represented using the same number of equal rows, just as the ants are marching in rows to get to a picnic. Using an array, the problem 3 × 4 would be represented as three rows of four.

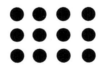

As we've seen with three rows of four, the related conceptual language translation would be ____ rows of ____. Although we are still working with equal "groups," the groups are now represented as rows of an array.

Table 3.4

Operation	Model	Conceptual Language
Multiplication	Equal Groups; Equal Distances	_____ groups of _____ "jumps" of ____
	Array	_____ rows of ____

Area Model

A third model for multiplication is the area model. In this case we represent multiplication as the area of a rectangle with the given dimensions. For 3 × 4 we would find the area of a rectangle with the dimensions three by four.

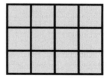

The area model can be used to represent single-digit multiplication. But it is also helpful for representing multi-digit multiplication (e.g., 13 × 24 or 134 × 372). I'd hate to watch students try to draw thirteen groups or rows of twenty-four let alone 134 groups of 372. It would be painful. But I wouldn't mind if students thought of a rectangle with dimensions thirteen by twenty-four.

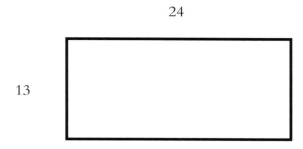

I admit, watching students draw and/or count all of those individual squares would also be painful. A more efficient technique is needed. If students understood that an area can be divided into sections, they can find the area of each section and then combine the areas to get the area of the total rectangle. What if I partition the above rectangle as shown below?

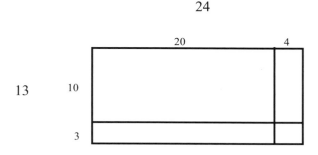

I can then find the area of each of the smaller rectangles. The area of a rectangle that is 10 by 20 is 200, 10 by 4 is 40, 3 by 20 is 60, and 3 by 4 is 12.

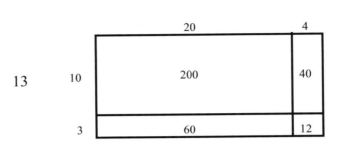

Using this area model representation we see that the area of a rectangle that is thirteen by twenty-four is 312. We thought of thirteen as ten and three, 13 = 10 + 3. We thought of twenty-four as twenty and four, 24 = 20 + 4. The product of thirteen and twenty-four is the same as the product of ten put together with three and twenty put together with four.

$$13 \times 24 = (10 + 3)(20 + 4)$$
$$= 200 + 60 + 40 + 12$$

We have another representation of the Distributive Property.

Remember the beauty of the Distributive Property? It is not limited to whole number multiplication. Consequently, the area model can also be used to represent mixed number multiplication (e.g., 2 ½ × 3 ½).

3½

	3	½
2	6	1
⅓	1	⅙

2⅓

The product of two and a third and three and a half is eight and a sixth.

$$2 \tfrac{1}{3} \times 3 \tfrac{1}{2} = (2 + \tfrac{1}{3})(3 + \tfrac{1}{2})$$
$$= 8 \tfrac{1}{6}$$

This looks a bit different from the arithmetic technique I was taught. Following the steps of that algorithm, I would rewrite 2 ⅓ as ⅞ and 3 ½ as ⁷⁄₂. I would find the product of seven-thirds and seven-halves by multiplying the numerators and denominators, $^{49}\!/_6$. I would then rewrite $^{49}\!/_6$ as the mixed number $8\,^1\!/_6$. Instead, the area model represents an algebraic approach to multiplication using the Distributive Property.

This model is not restricted to the elementary grades. In algebra, many students will use algebra tiles and the area model to represent binomial multiplication.

$$(x + 2)(x + 3)$$

Within the algebra tile set there are tiles with dimensions x by x, 1 by x, and 1 by 1.

We could also represent $(x + 2)(x + 3)$ using the same approach as we used for 13 by 24, simplifying the drawing.

$$(x + 2)(x + 3) = x^2 + 3x + 2x + 6$$
$$= x^2 + 5x + 6$$

In each of the above cases we thought of multiplication as finding the area of rectangles with the given dimensions, ____ by ____. This context provides us with another way to translate multiplication expressions.

Table 3.5

Operation	Model	Conceptual Language
Multiplication	Equal Groups; Equal Distances	_____ groups of _____ "jumps" of _____
	Array	_____ rows of _____
	Area	_____ by _____ (dimensions of a rectangle)

Scaling

To this point I've avoided the use of the word "times." Times, as we saw in Chapter 2, would typically be seen as a word used to decode the symbols, 3 × 4. That is true in the early grades, but as students begin to investigate ratio and examine proportional relationships, they will be given contexts in which something may be three times larger or a three times smaller (a third of something). In this case "times" becomes a conceptual language translation for that multiplicative relationship of scaling (Otto et al., 2011).

Table 3.6

Operation	Model	Conceptual Language
Multiplication	Equal Groups; Equal Distances	_____ groups of _____ "jumps" of _____
	Array	_____ rows of _____
	Area	_____ by _____ (dimensions of a rectangle)
	Scaling	_____ times larger _____ times smaller

As with the division models, it is important for students to understand and use each of these models for multiplication. The multiplication representations of equal groups, equal jumps, equal rows, rectangular area, and scaling are similar to the contexts students will see in word problems. These models also provide potential conceptual language translations.

Subtraction

Removal

As with multiplication and division, there are a number of ways in which we can think about subtraction (Carpenter et al., 1999; Caldwell et al., 2011). The model that has received the most attention is subtraction as removal or take away. When thinking of subtraction in this way the conceptual language translation is pretty straightforward. We would translate 5 − 3 as five take away three or five remove three. Most students are familiar with this translation. This model for subtraction is used in many story problems and provides us with one of the conceptual translations for subtraction.

Table 3.7

Operation	Model	Conceptual Language
Subtraction	Removal	_____ remove _____
		_____ take away _____

Comparison

But subtraction is not always removal. It can also involve comparisons. That is, we could also think of 5 − 3 as the relationship between three and five.

From this drawing we see that five is two more than three. The possible language translations would be,

- ◆ How many more than three is five?
- ◆ Five is how many more than three?
- ◆ How many fewer than five is three?
- ◆ Three is how many fewer than five?

Notice that with this last translation we are not reading left to right. We are also using the terms "more" and "fewer" instead of relying on greater than and less than.

With comparison subtraction we may actually be thinking in terms of addition. Consider the phrase, "How many more than three is five?" I used this phrase to represent 5 − 3. But I could also think of this as a missing addend problem.

$$3 + \underline{\quad} = 5$$

You may find that students are thinking in terms of addition as they compare three and five. That's okay. After all, subtraction and addition are inverses.

When building understandings of the operations using conceptual translations, we must be flexible in our reading of the expressions and equations. This is especially true when thinking of subtraction as comparison. This subtraction model provides additional conceptual translations for subtraction: how many more, how many fewer.

Table 3.8

Operation	Model	Conceptual Language
Subtraction	Removal	_____ remove _____ _____ take away _____
	Comparison	How many more than _____ is _____? How many fewer than _____ is _____ rows of _____? _____ is how many fewer than _____? _____ is how many more than _____?

Difference as Distance

Difference is the term we use for the answer to a subtraction problem. However, difference is also a conceptual term for subtraction. It is a type of comparison. For our purposes we'll think of subtraction as a distance. For example, we would think of 5 – 3 as how far apart are five and three? Two.

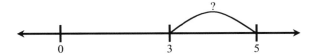

The tricky thing with this model is that distance is always positive and we know that subtraction does not always result in a positive answer. It is directional. If we subtract a smaller number from a larger number, we get a positive result. If we subtract a larger number from a smaller number, we get a negative result. With our problem, 5 – 3, the difference between five and three is two, 5 – 3 = 2. But if we reverse the order, 3 – 5, the difference between three and five is negative two, 3 – 5 = –2.

This model for subtraction helps me think about integer subtraction a bit differently. Consider the problems, 4 – (–5) and –5 – 4. One of these will have a negative result and the other a positive result. If we think of difference as the distance between these two values, how far apart are four and negative five?

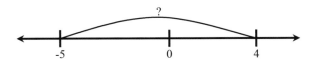

Those values are nine apart. Which of these expressions, 4 − (−5) or −5 − 4, will result in a negative difference? Remember that we get a negative result when we subtract a larger number from a smaller number. Four is larger than negative five so the difference between negative five and four, −5 − 4, is negative nine, −9.

$$-5 - 4 = -9$$

The difference between four and negative five, 4 − (−5), is nine, 9.

$$4 - (-5) = 9$$

In each case we're thinking of difference as a distance between numbers. You may be thinking, "That's a little confusing." Give it time.

One of the other key understandings related to difference is that there are an infinite number of ways to make the same difference. How many ways could you make a difference of four? 8 − 4, 7 − 3, and 6 − 2 are just three of the ways. Are you thinking, "Yeah, so what?" Can you picture a little arc between eight and four on a number line?

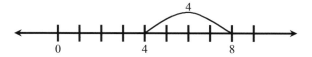

Now slide that arc to the left one unit and it is between seven and three.

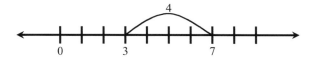

One more unit to the left and the arc is between six and two.

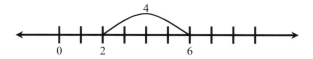

Now let's think about an arc between 400 and 137, to represent 400 − 137. Using an arithmetic approach we would need to regroup . . . twice. But slide that arc one unit to the left, 400 − 137 is the same as 399 − 136. The first, 400 − 137, requires multiple regrouping. The second, 399 − 136, requires no regrouping. Thinking of difference as distance is a powerful subtraction model.

Table 3.9

Operation	Model	Conceptual Language
Subtraction	Removal	_____ remove _____ _____ take away _____
	Comparison	How many more than _____ is _____? How many fewer than _____ is _____ rows of _____? _____ is how many fewer than _____? _____ is how many more than _____?
	Difference (difference as a distance between values)	The difference between _____ and _____. (Thinking . . . how far apart are _____ and _____)

As with division and multiplication, fluency with just one of these models is not sufficient for building conceptual understandings of subtraction. Each of these models represents the contexts of subtraction and students should be comfortable with each model and the associated language.

Addition

As we've seen with each of the other operations, the models for addition provide us with the associated conceptual language as well as addition contexts for story problems. I find the models for addition a bit easier than for the other operations. That's a bit odd since the other operations are related to addition. Think about it. Subtraction is the inverse of addition. We can actually "think addition" to solve. Multiplication is a specialized form of addition. Division is the inverse of multiplication or it can be thought of as repeated subtraction (the inverse of addition). Hmmm! It seems that each of the operations are related to one another. That is an important conceptual understanding.

There are two primary models for addition (Carpenter et al., 1999; Caldwell et al., 2011). One involves the action of joining or combining. The other involves the relationship of parts to a whole or total. As with each of the other operations, these models give us the related conceptual language translations.

Joining

Joining things or putting things together is a common context for thinking about addition. This will give you a hint regarding my age but I have a collection of photo albums. The old printed photos are something I treasure. But the photo albums are not full. I'd like to get rid of some of the albums if possible. They are bulky. I know I could scan the photos and be done with the albums altogether, but it's not the same. There's just something about that paper. They're antiques . . . as am I. I can take the photos from one album and put them together with the photos in another album. I'm combining the two groups of photos. If I'm lucky I can take photos from a third album and join them with the other two. One hundred thirty-two photos put together with fifty-six photos is 188 photos in that single album, 132 + 56 = 188. One album gone. Woo hoo!

Table 3.10

Operation	Model	Conceptual Language
Addition	Joining or Combining	____ joined with ____ ____ put together with ____ ____ combined with ____

Part-Part-Total

There are other contexts in which I may want to know the total but I'm not actually combining the groups. In the town I live in there is a family that has several car dealerships. They own a Ford dealership, a Toyota dealership, and a Nissan dealership. I could determine the total number of cars in their inventory without putting them all together on a single lot. I confess. In my mind I think of putting the quantities of cars at each dealership together to determine the total. But I realize I'm not combining the actual sets together.

For children this may involve a problem in which they find the total number of students in their class when given the number of boys and the number of girls, or when told there are twenty-four children in a class, fourteen of which are boys. They are to find the number of girls.

Table 3.11

Operation	Model	Conceptual Language
Addition	Joining or Combining	____ joined with ____ ____ put together with ____ ____ combined with ____
	Part-Part-Total Part-Part-Whole	____ and ____

Understanding the meanings of the operations and the associated models and conceptual language gives students access to what at first sight may look like a complex mathematical idea. Using an equal grouping model we can introduce students to the Distributive Property. In understanding difference as distance, students can use equivalent differences to solve 400 − 137 and later use this concept for integer subtraction.

The meanings of the operations and related models provide us with related conceptual language translations. The conceptual language translations represent the language and context of word problems. Each of these is an important component for building conceptual understandings and creating a language-rich math class.

Questions for Reflection

1. What are your students' current understandings of the operations?
2. With which specific models are your students most comfortable?
3. Which, if any, models need to be introduced or strengthened?
4. What specific strategies will you use to incorporate operation models and conceptual language use into your daily mathematics investigations?

References

Caldwell, J. H., Karp, K., & Bay-Williams, J. M. (2011). *Developing Essential Understanding of Addition and Subtraction. Pre-K—Grade 2*. Reston, VA: NCTM.

Carpenter, T. P., Fennema, E., Franke, M. L., Levi, L., & Empson, S. B. (1999). *Children's Mathematics. Cognitively Guided Instruction*. Portsmouth, NH: Heinemann.

Chapin S. H. & Johnson, A. (2006). *Math Matters. Grades K-8 Understanding the Math You Teach*. Sausalito, CA: Math Solutions Publications.

Daro, P. (2014, August 1). *Phil Daro Against Answer Getting SD* (YouTube Video). Retrieved from https://www.youtube.com/watch?v=DgTnmRyV9bc

Hutchins, P. (1986). *The Doorbell Rang*. New York, NY: Greenwillow Books.

National Council of Teachers of Mathematics (1989). *Curriculum and Evaluation Standards for School Mathematics*. Reston, VA: NCTM.

National Council of Teachers of Mathematics (2000). *Principles and Standards for School Mathematics*. Reston, VA: NCTM.

National Governors Association Center for Best Practices & Council of Chief State School Officers. (2010). *Common Core State Standards for Mathematics*. Washington, DC: Authors.

Otto, A. D., Caldwell, J. H., Lubinski, C. A., & Hancock, S. W. (2011). *Developing Essential Understandings of Multiplication and Division. Grades 3–5*. Reston, VA: NCTM.

Pinczes, E. J. (1993). *One Hundred Hungry Ants*. Boston, MA: Houghton Mifflin Company.

4

Tips for Creating a Language-Rich Math Class

You never know where you'll find inspiration. A colleague once shared a conversation she had with a young student. They had been talking for a while when he turned and said, "What do you know?" You might be able to guess what her side of the conversation may have been. Ever since I heard that story it's been my goal . . . to have students wonder what I do know.

To me, a language-rich class is one in which the conversations do not all go through me (Corwin, 1996). They happen between students. One of my favorite examples of this occurred in a fourth-grade class. We were investigating angle relationships. I had drawn a right angle and a sixty-degree angle on two sheets of large paper. I placed them in the center of our circle and asked which angle was larger. Almost all of the students said the right angle was larger.

Without giving it much thought I had drawn each of the angles with the rays approximately the same length. A colleague in the room noticed. She asked what would happen if we lengthened one of the rays of the sixty-degree angle. Great question! I did. Would you be surprised to hear that some of the students said that it was now larger than the right angle? They were closing in the third side and comparing the areas. Who knew? Remember Celia from Chapter 1 and twenty-four hours in a day but not knowing how long night is yet? Here was another example of the importance of asking from a different angle . . . so to speak.

The students began to discuss whether the sixty-degree angle was bigger or if it was still smaller than the right angle. There were some great conversations. Students were trying to convince each other that their answer was correct and to change the minds of those who didn't agree. My favorite moment occurred when one of the boys was trying to convince his classmate that the size of the angle hadn't changed. He placed a protractor at the vertex and asked his classmate what it said. She replied sixty degrees. He then took a meter stick and closed in the third side and again asked her the measure of the angle. She again replied sixty degrees. He asked her if she could see that it hadn't changed. She said no. He very respectfully slid the paper and materials toward her and said, "Then show me how it has changed." Now on the outside I remained calm, but on the inside I was jumping up and down yelling, "Yes! Yes! Yes! This is fantastic!" Talk about critiquing the reasoning of a peer and trying to provide a convincing argument . . . a language-rich math moment. Amazing!

There are a number of simple techniques that can be used to create these language-rich math moments.

Consider Sitting Down

Changing your physical location can change the flow of the conversation. Did you notice that for the angle lesson we were sitting in a circle . . . on the floor? It was amazing that after a short amount of time the students quit looking to me to lead the conversation and started discussing ideas with one another. This also happens when I sit down with the students and encourage them to talk directly with their peers.

Are You Sure? How Did You Get Your Answer?

Have you ever asked students "How do you know?" or "How did you get that?" and they immediately change their answer? They don't answer the question but assume that their answer must be wrong. It says a great deal about their previous experiences in math class. More than likely, incorrect answers were greeted with those same questions. Consequently, students quickly change their answers. They may even start guessing. Unfortunately, they don't defend.

We want to change that dynamic. Have students first lead with how they got an answer instead of the answer itself. Then ask them if they are sure and have them defend, whether the answer is correct or incorrect. Have students always defend their thinking. Defense becomes the expectation.

Don't Be the Answer Key

As we know, many students look to the teacher to confirm that they are "doing it right." Some check in with each step of the solution. Many students are very adept at reading our faces. They know that we cue with our face and with other gestures. Students expect this. They are focused on trying to tell us what they think we want to hear instead of telling us what they think.

Remember the child who asked, "What do you know?" The teacher definitely wasn't his answer key. He was doing all of the work trying to explain everything to her. Exactly . . . language rich! When we cue with our face we are listening for what we hope to hear. We have a specific instructional path in mind. But if we can put on an interested face, a curious face, or a confused face, students will more likely tell us what they think. I find them to be very chatty. This in turn gives us insight into their mathematical understandings and creates language-rich math moments.

Investigations to Try and Questions for Reflection

1. Notice how often your students look to you for the answers. What strategies could you implement to get students to defend their thinking and become confident in their answers?
2. Ask your students how they know, how they got an answer, or why they think that and see if they change their answer or defend their thinking. What are some strategies that can be used to change the expectations to presenting and defending solutions . . . correct or incorrect?

Ask a Question to Help Them Change Their Minds

We're sitting down. We're getting students to always defend their answers. We are not cueing with our face because we're not the answer key. But how do we get students to have those "angle" conversations?

Debriefing a lesson takes many forms. A common technique is for students to share and defend their solutions. If the solution is incorrect, hands shoot up. Other students want to share and defend the "correct" solution. We can change this dynamic by saying, "Don't tell me what you think the answer is. Ask him (or her) a question to help him change his mind." When you first try this don't be surprised by looks of shock and confusion . . . and hands going down. You've just caused them to think quite differently. They have to critique the reasoning of others and think of a question that will help their peers reconsider their thinking. Give it time. The hands will come back up. The question the student asks may or may not work, but the level of thought just increased. Don't be surprised if you get more statements than questions at first. I remember a student who turned to his classmate and said, "Please change your mind."

Think, Pair, Share—Tell Me What Your Partner Said

Getting students to listen to and value what their peers have to say is key to building a language-rich classroom. I love the think-pair-share strategy. I think it is a great tool for increasing the dialogue between students and it is a great assessment tool for me.

If you aren't familiar with this technique, students are given individual THINK time. This is especially important for our second-language learners and students who have language-processing challenges. It gives them time to interpret what has been asked. It also lets all children know that mathematics is about thoughtfulness, not speed. Students are then asked to talk with a partner (PAIR). We just increased the number of students who are talking from the few who share during whole-class discussions to almost all. I admit that some students dominate these turn-and-talk moments. Others prefer to hitchhike and some may not understand what has been asked. I tell the students ahead of time that when we discuss as a whole group I will ask them to share what their partner said, not what they said. Students who may not have understood what was asked or are not sure of the language now have something to share. Those who love to share are encouraged to ask their partner questions. Knowing that they must share what their partner said develops a need to listen to and value what their peers have to say. When you begin using this technique you may need to give students additional time to listen to their peers. The last step is to have the students SHARE what their partners said with the class.

I use this with students from kindergarten through the middle grades. It is fun to do in kindergarten. I often have a student describe what her partner said while the partner is shaking her head saying, "I didn't say that!" Remember to be patient and to give students time to describe their thinking. There may be false starts, "I forgots," and missteps, but over the course of the year young children will become better listeners and better at using mathematical language to describe their thinking.

Encourage students to ask one another questions to change their peers' minds, then sit down on the edge of the group. How does the dynamic of the conversation change? What strategies could you use to get the students to talk to one another?

Have Students Use Four Representations (Concrete, Pictorial, Verbal, Symbolic) Whenever Possible

We are all familiar with symbolic representations in mathematics. My school mathematics experiences primarily consisted of manipulating these symbolic representations, $400 - 137$, 13×24, $42 \div 6$, $x + 5 = 12$, $xy > 0$. As we've discussed in previous chapters, conceptual language provides an alternative representation for the symbols. The models for the operations inform the conceptual language we use as well as pictorial representations. Concrete representations are the fourth. Whenever possible, I try to have students represent mathematics in these four ways: concrete (build it), pictorial (draw it), verbal (spoken and written using conceptual language), and symbols (Perry & Atkins, 2002).

Concrete	Pictorial
Verbal	Symbolic

As I plan the students' mathematical experiences, I think of the ways in which each of these representations can be included. As students transition from using concrete materials, they are still expected to use the other three representations.

Let's revisit Lesa's kindergarten class working on Farmer Joe's potato problem. The children used concrete materials to separate the twenty potatoes into four equal groups. The children could then draw a picture of their solution, before or after the "hocus pocus." We used fair share language. If we move up a few grades, third-graders could begin the same way. They may use blocks to represent the potatoes and draw a picture of their solution. We would use the language of separating into four equal groups or same sized groups and then connect to the symbolic representation, $20 \div 4 = 5$.

Investigation to Try and Questions for Reflection

Choose an upcoming mathematics topic. Determine the ways in which the four representations will be used and connected each day.

1. What did you learn about your students' understandings?
2. Did you observe students who seemed more comfortable with one of the representations and struggled with others?
3. What additional experiences are needed to increase students' comfort with all four representations?

Conceptual Language vs. Symbolic Decoding

Remember to use conceptual language translations at least 90% of the time and symbolic decoding less than 10% of the time when reading symbolic representations. This is especially true when computing. Conceptual language translations will connect the meaning of the operations with the symbolic representations. An added benefit is that this builds and reinforces the language of word problems when there is a symbolic focus.

Building and Using Language

The National Council of Teachers of Mathematics' (2000) *Principals and Standards for School Mathematics* and the *Common Core State Standards for Mathematics* (National Governors Association Center for Best Practices & Council of Chief State School Officers, 2010) emphasize the importance of presenting arguments and critiquing the reasoning of others. The NCTM Standards also highlight attention to precision when using mathematical symbols, language, and other representations. Students are expected to be fluent in their understanding of mathematical concepts and their ability to explain and defend their understandings and conclusions. This requires a level of sophistication in the use of mathematical language.

This level of sophistication is not developed in a periodic language lesson or on special math days. It involves:

- ◆ Precise mathematical language used daily during math class time and in other mathematical situations;
- ◆ Children describing and defending their thinking;
- ◆ Allowing students to experience false starts and to struggle with the language; and
- ◆ Practice using precise language; connecting concrete, pictorial, verbal, and symbolic representations; and hearing the language used by their classmates.

We need to find a way to sit down, be quiet, and make them wonder what we **do** know.

Questions for Reflection

When students have a misconception or are struggling, we often think, "How can I explain it so that they understand?" Instead, consider the questions you can ask or the experiences that are lacking or are needed. Essentially, whenever you want to tell them something, ask a question instead. Describe a misunderstanding that one of your students has. What question(s) could you ask to help him rethink? What experiences is he lacking or are needed?

References

Corwin, R. B. (1996). *Talking Mathematics*. Portsmouth, NH: Heinemann.

National Council of Teachers of Mathematics (2000). *Principles and Standards for School Mathematics*. Reston, VA: NCTM.

National Governors Association Center for Best Practices & Council of Chief State School Officers. (2010). *Common Core State Standards for Mathematics*. Washington, DC: Authors.

Perry, J. A. & Atkins, S. L. (2002). It's not just notation: Valuing children's representations. *Teaching Children Mathematics, 9*(4), 196–201.

5

Purposefully Choose and Use Materials

Have you ever taught a unit using manipulative materials or games that you thought were great, but later you learned that the students didn't quite understand what you had hoped? Or when the students were asked questions on a test or after some time had passed they didn't do well? Were you thinking, "We spent so much time on this. What happened?" Perhaps they didn't recognize what they were being asked or didn't connect it to what they had previously done. We know that covered does not equate with learned. However, I remember a professor saying to me, "It can't just be hands-on. It has to be minds-on." I wondered how much of what I was doing was only hands-on.

Subitizing

To be able to effectively operate on numbers, students need a strong number sense. We know that a key element of number sense is subitizing (Wright, Martland, & Stafford, 2000). Subitizing is the ability to recognize and name a quantity without counting. We do this without thinking when we play board games. Do you need to stop and count the pips on a die or do you just know a five when you see it?

We also want children to be able to quickly recognize these quantities. Subitizing domino dot, five-frame, ten-frame, and random combinations provides students with visual images that move students from counting to working with quantities as their primary strategy for computing.

One activity for helping students subitize domino dot images is to have them play a simple matching game with dominoes. The version I've always used involves students playing in groups of three or four. With the dominoes all facing down, each player selects seven dominoes. The player with the highest double starts the game. We give doubles a special place of honor by turning them perpendicular to the rest of the dominoes in the train. Each player takes turns adding one domino to an end of the train. They may not add to the middle so there are only two choices for each turn.

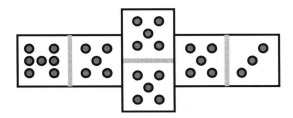

If a player doesn't have a play, not to worry; they draw from the pile until they do. After all, every player should have a turn. Play continues until a player uses all of his dominoes.

It's a fun game. Kids like playing it. But here's the thing: Have you ever watched kids play dominoes? The images for each quantity are identical. A five always looks like:

And a six like:

Children can quickly match the visual images without knowing it's a five or six or . . . . I have the intended goal of students' subitizing domino dot images one to nine. I run the risk of falling short of this goal because students are matching the images without naming them. They are hands-on but they are not minds-on . . . or at least not focused on what I'd hoped.

There is a simple fix. Have the students name the quantity they are matching. If they play a double have them name it "double ____." In our case I would have said, "double five." The doubles are a key strategy used in both addition and multiplication so it is important that they have internalized pictorial images of doubles. At first you may see them counting the pips but they will eventually become fluent at naming domino dot quantities without counting . . . subitizing.

This purposeful approach to how we use mathematical materials can help build conceptual depth and mathematical language, but so can the purposeful selection of the material itself. What if we substitute ten-frame dominoes for classic dominoes? The ten-frame dominoes I use do not have identical arrangements for each quantity one to nine. Below are three examples of arrangements for eight.

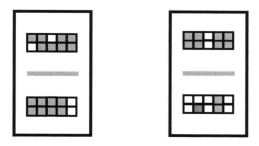

Students must match the quantities—not specific arrangements. In this case the goal is for students to understand that any time there are two empty spaces it will be eight. Two fewer than ten is eight. Let's return to our simple matching version of dominoes.

Ten-Frame Domino Match

Materials: Ten-frame dominoes
Players: Groups of three or four

1. Mix up dominoes well and place upside down.
2. Each player selects seven dominoes.
3. The player with the highest double starts. Doubles are placed perpendicular to the other dominoes in the train.
4. Players take turns placing a domino at the end of the train. Players must name the quantity they are matching. If it is a double, they will name the double.

5. If a player does not have a play, he draws from the pile until he does. After all, everyone should have a turn.

Goal: Be the first to get rid of your dominoes.

Sound familiar? It should. It is the same game I described for classic dominoes. But these ten-frame dominoes allow us to add one more critical component to the game . . . a defense. Not defense versus offense but defense as in defending your answer. Remember the arrangements are not identical. When players make a play, they must say the quantity they are matching and how they know they match. For example, let's say the following domino is at the end of the train.

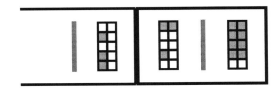

I'm going to match the eight.

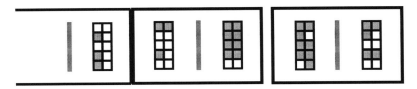

I would say, "Eight. I know because double four is eight and two fewer than ten is eight." When I introduce the game, I invite the students to suggest ways in which I could defend a match. I encourage students to suggest a variety of possibilities.

There is more language development and language use involved with this material choice than with classic dominoes. The only restriction: counting is not a defense. As your students play the above game, change Step 4 to read, "Players take turns placing a domino at the end of the train. Players must name and defend the quantity they are matching."

I've described the game using whole numbers but I could just as easily have called the dominoes "tenths-frame dominoes." Let's reexamine the last example. If I were playing tenths-frame match I would say, "eight-tenths. I know because double four-tenths is eight-tenths and two-tenths fewer than ten-tenths is eight-tenths."

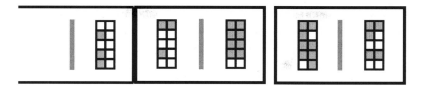

As we try to meet the needs of all students, one challenge is to find ways to increase the cognitive demand (Hess, 2006) for some students while giving other students the gift of time to understand and internalize concepts. By purposely choosing the appropriate materials and being strategic in assigning student groups and the directions given, we can do just that.

Increasing the Cognitive Demand of the Experience

We start the class playing Ten-Frame (or Tenths-Frame) Domino Match. The goal is for students to fluently name and describe how they know they have a match in a variety of ways. This may include using doubles and near doubles,

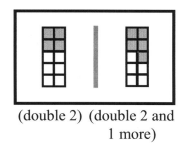

(double 2) (double 2 and
1 more)

describing the relationship to five,

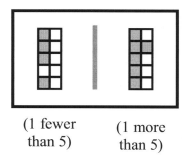

(1 fewer   (1 more
than 5)   than 5)

describing the relationship to ten,

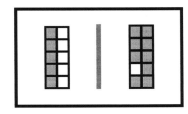

(half of 10)   (1 fewer
than 10)

or part-part-totals.

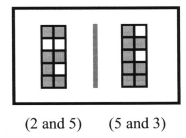

(2 and 5)   (5 and 3)

Not by counting!

Number fluency will occur at different times for different students. I use a phased approach to increase the cognitive demand for some while others are building fluency within a phase. Consider Ten-Frame (Tenths-Frame) Domino Match as Phase 1.

Combinations for Ten

Once students are comfortable naming and defending the quantities they are matching using the ten-frame (tenths-frame) dominoes transition them to Phase 2. In Phase 2, instead of players matching quantities, students will combine two quantities to make a total of ten. Bridging to ten is an important addition strategy in the early grades but don't let the name fool you. It is actually the Associative Property. We want students to know that eight and five is the same as ten and three.

$$8 + 5 = 10 + 3$$

We talk about bridging to ten or making ten. But let's look at it another way. I can think of five as two put together with three. So,

$$8 + 5 = 8 + (2 + 3)$$

Instead of associating the two with the three, we will associate it with the eight.

$$8 + 5 = 8 + (2 + 3)$$
$$= (8 + 2) + 3$$
$$\text{so, } 8 + 5 = 10 + 3.$$

Pictorially,

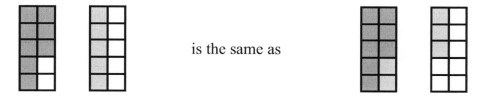

is the same as

We fill the first frame with two from the second frame. Again, if I'm using these as tenths frames I've shown, eight-tenths and five-tenths is the same as one and three-tenths.

$$.8 + 5 = 1 + 3$$

Phase 2: Making Ten with Ten Frames—Building Addition Conceptual Language

Materials: Ten-frame dominoes (remove any dominoes with a blank frame on a side)

Players: Small groups of three or four

1. Place dominoes upside-down and mix well.
2. Each player selects seven dominoes.
3. The player with a domino that totals ten begins. For example,

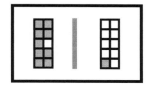

If no one has a domino totaling ten, select from the pile and use that domino to start the game. It would just be cruel to have the first player draw from the pile until they find a domino that totals ten.

In this phase we are developing fluency with translations for addition and equality.

Table 5.1

+	=
put together	same as
combine	is
join with	
and	

4. Players take turns placing a domino at either end of the train.

    Note: There are only two options for each play. Players must describe the combination they have made and how they know. Suppose I begin play with:

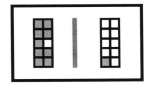

I would say, "Nine joined with one is the same as ten. One put together with nine is ten. I know because that one (pointing to the one) can slide in there (pointing to the empty space) to total ten."
Suppose that Player 2 has a double nine.

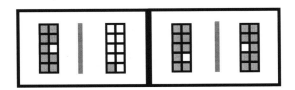

Notice that we do not highlight the double in this game. It is the "sections" that are touching that must total ten. Player 2 could say, "One and nine is ten. Nine combined with one is the same as ten. I know because this one will slide in there."

    Note: Encourage students to use a variety of conceptual language translations to describe addition and equality. Notice that "makes" is not on the list as a translation for equality. "Makes" infers the answer comes next. One misunderstanding of equality is, "now write the answer." We want to develop equality as a balance. In later phases students will begin with the total, ten.

5. If a player does not have a play, she draws from the pile until she does. After all, everyone should have a turn.
6. The goal is to be the first to get rid of your dominoes.

Mathematically, students are working with missing addends and combinations to make ten. As students become fluent with using conceptual language to describe the combinations and can defend the combinations, transition them to Phase 3 . . . the recording phase.

Phase 3: **Recording**

For each of these phases we add to the previous phase. In the previous phase, students were connecting pictorial and verbal representations as well as defending their combinations for ten. In this phase students will connect these two representations to a symbolic representation. Timing is everything. I try to be a stickler in having students precisely follow these steps. I hope you'll see the value in it too.

1. Place dominoes upside-down and mix well.
2. Each player selects seven dominoes.
3. The player with a domino that totals ten begins.
4. Each player places a domino at one end of the train. As the player describes the combinations, all of the group members record what is said . . . **as it is said**.
5. All players must record at the same time. The player whose turn it is will write as he describes the combinations. The other players will write as they hear the descriptions. We are trying to create a strong connection between the verbal and symbolic representations. We do not want students saying the combinations and then writing. For the other players no hitchhiking or looking over and writing what they see. Remember we are trying to help students connect the symbolic representations with the conceptual translations.
6. Looking at the previous example, I place my domino at the end of the train. I say,

"Nine put together with one is the same as ten"

As I write,   9   +   1   =   10

I write the "9" as I say "nine." I write "+" as I say "put together." I write "1" as I say "one." I write "=" as I say "is the same as." And

I write "10" as I say "ten." My group members are writing at the same time as I'm describing the combination. Each member is either writing as they say the relationship or writing as they hear it.

I also say the turnaround "fact".

"One joined with nine is the same as ten"

As we write,　1　　　+　　　9　　　=　　　10

Remember, it's not just about writing equations to show combinations of ten and the Commutative Property. Have you ever tried to write "+" while you're saying "put together" or "joined with"? How about "=" as you're saying "same as"? It's not easy but that's the connection we need students to have. Keep an eye on them.

Note: If playing the decimal version it would be,

Verbal:　　Nine-tenths put together with one-tenth is the same as ten-tenths

or one

Symbolic
Recording:　.9　　　　　+　　　　　.1　　　　　=　　　　　1.0

Phase 3B: Phase 3 with the Defense Added

Once students are comfortable with the timing involved in connecting conceptual language with symbolic recording, ask them to end with a defense. After all have recorded the two equations, the player would continue with, "I know because I can slide that one in there to make a total of ten." If playing tenths-frame dominoes, the player would continue with, "I know because I can slide one-tenth in there to make a total of ten-tenths or one."

Phase 4: Begin with the Total

Everything is the same as in Phase 3, but in this phase we'll add another step. In this phase players will describe and record in four ways.

"Nine put together with one is the same as ten"

As we write,　9　　　　+　　　　1　　　　=　　　　10

"One joined with nine is the same as ten"

As we write,　1　　　+　　　9　　　　=　　　　10

"Ten is the same as nine combined with one"

As we write, 10   =   9   +   1

"Ten is the same as one put together with nine"

As we write, 10   =   1   +   9

Phase 4B: Phase 4 with the Defense Added

Once students are comfortable with the timing involved in connecting conceptual language with symbolic recording, ask them to end with a defense. After all have recorded the four equations, the player would continue with, "I know because I can slide that one in there to make a total of ten." If playing tenths-frame dominoes, the player would continue with, "I know because I can slide one-tenth in there to make a total of ten-tenths or one."

In Phases 2–4 the focus has been on combining two parts to make a total of ten and connecting pictorial, verbal, and symbolic representations. Mathematically, students are solving missing addend problems. The ten frame provides a visual cue. We are having students look at what is filled as well as what is missing. This would not happen with classic dominoes.

Phase 5: Two or Three Sections to Total Ten: Verbal, Pictorial, Symbolic

This phase is the same as Phase 4, but in Phase 5 students can combine two or three "sections" to make a total of ten. Let's say it's my turn. I look at each end of the train and there is a four showing. I look at my remaining dominoes. No six. I look at the pile. If you've had to draw from the pile, it's not something you look forward to. But now in this new phase I can use the domino that has a one on one side and a five on the other.

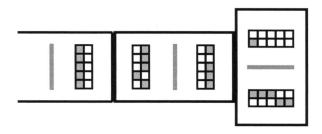

"Four and five put together with one is ten."

Can you think of three additional ways to describe the combinations, two of which start with the total ten? I could say,

"One combined with four joined with five is ten."
"Ten is the same as five joined with one combined with four."
Ten is the same as four and five joined with one."

What are the other possibilities?

Notice that for each of these I didn't combine the five and one to use six in the equations. I chose to leave it as three addends. The next player now has several options. She could play off of the five to have five put together with five is the same as ten (a missing addend problem).

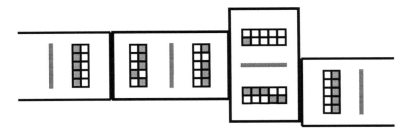

She could play off of the one to have one and nine is the same as ten.

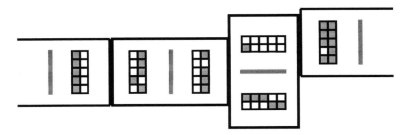

She could combine the one and five to get six, and play a domino with four on a side.

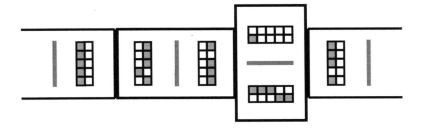

Remember that it is the sections that are touching that must total five. You may choose to split Phase 5 into two parts. First have students focus on building the verbal-pictorial connection. Once fluent, add the recording-symbolic link.

Let's return to my last turn in which I had three sections touching to make a total of ten.

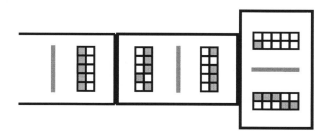

Remember the timing is important. I place my domino at the end of the train. I then say,

"Five put together with one joined with four is the same as ten"

As I write, 5   +   1   +   4   =   10

The other members of my group also write the equation as I'm using conceptual language to describe.

"One combined with four joined with five is ten"

As we write, 1   +   4   +   5   =   10

"Ten is the same as five joined with one combined with four"

As we write, 10   =   5   +   1   +   4

"Ten is the same as four and five joined with one"

As we write, 10   =   4   +   5   +   1

Think of how the math has changed. In Phases 2–4 students were solving missing addend problems. In this phase students are still finding the missing addend. But they may also consider part-part-total combinations for the missing addend. If we look at the domino I played during my last turn we'll see that the amount of imbedded practice has increased. The next player has two missing addend problems to consider: One and what is ten? Five and what is ten? They look at their dominoes and see that they don't have a six, a nine, or a five. They combine the one and five on my domino and get six (fact practice). They look and see that they have a four . . . another missing addend. That's just on one end of the train. They have another missing addend problem at the other end. If they can't make a total with ten with two sections touching, they are back to considering part-part-total relationships that are the same as the needed missing addend. Whew!

Phase 6: Two, Three, or Four Addends

We can take this one step further. In Phase 5, I showed three options the next player would have when I had three sections touching to make ten. But there is a fourth option. Let's say the next player didn't have a domino with a nine or a five. When she combined the one and five together to get six, she looked at her dominoes and saw she didn't have a domino with a four. Bummer! But she did have a one and a three. Remember, it's sections that are touching must total ten. She has it! She can have four addends to make a total of ten.

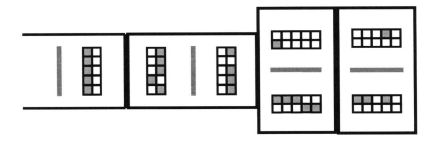

Just as with Phase 5, you may choose to have students first practice the verbal piece. In four ways they would describe the combinations they've made using conceptual language, two starting with the total of ten. In Phase 7 we add the recording component again.

Think of how the math has changed again. In Phases 2–4 students were solving missing addend problems. In Phase 5 students were still finding the missing addend. But they also considered part-part-total combinations for the missing addend. After I made my play, the next player had three missing addend problems to consider, a part-part-total problem, and then another missing addend problem. By adding a four-sections-touching option we've increased the amount of thinking and imbedded practice again. The next player can still ask: One and what is ten? Five and what is ten? He looks at his dominoes and sees that he doesn't have a six, a nine, or a five. He combines the one and five on my domino and gets six (fact practice). He looks and sees if he has a four . . . another missing addend. He doesn't. He now considers part-part-total relationships to make four. That's at one end of the train. There is a lot of thinking and practice involved in this game. Remember the defense! Whew!

Phase 7: Two, Three, or Four Sections to Total Ten: Verbal, Pictorial, Symbolic

This phase is the same as Phase 5 but players can also create combinations of four addends as described in Phase 6. The timing of saying and recording is still important. The players will describe and record in four ways.

Notice that each of the phases is designed to increase the cognitive demand of the students needing more challenge. I'm not expecting that all of the students progress through the stages at the same rate. I'm trying to provide the gift of time to students who need it to become fluent with the language, the defense of their choices, and the symbolic representations before moving onto the next phase. The goal is not for the students to complete all of the phases quickly; it's for students to feel comfortable with the conceptual language of addition, build a strong connection between that conceptual language and the related symbols, and build strong visual images of the filling of ten frames. Don't rush. Give them time to develop that fluency.

Although I gave detailed instructions about how to play this version of ten-frame (tenths-frame) dominoes, your students don't need to play this particular series of games. However, as you design games for students to play and complete activities, I hope you'll consider the following:

- What materials will you use?
- What will students say?
- What will the students write or draw?
- How will you have students connect the various representations?
- How will you have students defend their answers?
- How will you increase the cognitive demand of the tasks to meet the needs of all students?

Questions for Reflection

Think of a game your students currently play or an upcoming activity. Consider how you could use this phased approach to increase the cognitive demand for some students while giving others the gift of time to build fluency.

1. What materials will you use? Could a modification in materials increase opportunities for students to defend their thinking?
2. What will students say?

3. What will the students write or draw?
4. How will you have students connect the various representations?
5. How will you have students defend their answers?
6. How will you increase the cognitive demand of the tasks to meet the needs of all students?

Using Materials to Build Conceptual Understandings

When we think of using concrete materials we think of teaching concepts. But often manipulative materials are used to model procedures. Consider the ways in which base ten materials are used to teach subtraction. For a problem such as 62 – 29, students are taught to represent sixty-two using six tens and two ones. They may place the blocks on a work mat with the labels of "tens" and "ones" at the top.

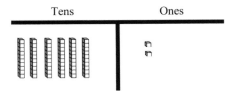

They are then taught to "trade in" one of the tens for ten ones because they don't have enough ones. When we use this approach, we are using concrete materials to teach the regrouping algorithm.

Let's say I'm buying an item that costs 29 cents. I happen to have six dimes and two pennies in my pocket. I can't remember a time that I said to the cashier, "I'd love to pay you but I don't have enough pennies. Could I trade you a dime for ten pennies?" Instead, I give the cashier three dimes and I hope that he knows he needs to give me a penny . . . without typing it into the cash register.

Suppose I asked students to show sixty-two using the fewest number of base ten pieces. We would still see,

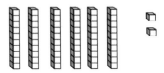

Instead of now teaching them how to remove twenty-nine using a specific procedure, what would happen if we asked the students to remove twenty-nine and stand back and watch? In this way we are focused on building an understanding of the removal model of subtraction and creating a problem

situation for them to solve. If you try this, you will be able to tell who has been taught the regrouping algorithm and who has not internalized that procedure. I see many students put back three of the tens and take a unit cube. They do what I did with the cashier.

Remember that we are trying to design experiences in which the students will connect a variety of representations. I sometimes begin with the concrete representation. At other times we begin with pictorial representations. In either case, I ask students to draw a picture to show sixty-two remove twenty-nine. Because students' drawings of the base ten rectangles all start to look alike, I have students use the following pictorial representations for the materials.

The students who remove three tens and "take back" one draw a picture that looks something like:

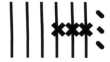

I've also seen students first remove twenty, then two. They know that they still need to remove seven more. They also know that ten can be separated into seven and three so they "cut" a ten and remove the seven that is still needed. Their drawing looks like the one below.

These students often use paper to hide the part of the ten-rod that they used when using concrete materials. Hmmm!

I've shared these two representations with many groups of teachers. I often hear, "I don't think my students could do that." Remember, I'm not teaching the students how to do this. I'm watching what they do and letting them present and defend their process to their peers. After one such discussion we decided to try this approach with a group of third-graders. I did not have them use the physical base ten materials but I did ask them to draw pictures to show their solution using the base ten representations shown above. As I walked around the room I noticed the first drawing on a student's paper. I asked her to draw her solution on the board. As she was walking to the front of the room, the student sitting across from her said, "I did it a different way." I looked. She had the second drawing on her paper. I've mentioned two-by-four moments. Another was about to happen.

As the teachers and I debriefed the lesson, I was told that the first little girl really struggled in mathematics. She had a very efficient strategy for subtracting twenty-nine but she was seen as a struggler in mathematics. How were we measuring success in mathematics? It made me think of the first student I observed using the second method years before. He had an individualized education plan (IEP) in mathematics, but boy could he problem solve and visualize numbers. He understood the meaning of subtraction and could represent efficient techniques for removing quantities consistently and accurately. When we allowed him access to mathematics through his strengths instead of forcing him to solve problems using a specific set of procedures, his weakness, he was very successful. He passed the state's high-stakes assessment with no assistance. The next year he was just a couple of points shy of advanced. He was considered to be the strongest math student in the class by his peers. Hmmm! Building conceptual understanding is very powerful.

Do you know who had the most difficulty drawing the pictures? The ones who tried to use the regrouping algorithm or the students who did a symbol-by-symbol drawing. The students who tried to pictorially represent the regrouping algorithm also began with six tens and two ones.

They "traded" a ten for ten ones by crossing out a ten and adding ten ones. At least that's what they tried to do. When I looked at the drawings of these students I saw two different pictures. Some of the students had drawn:

Others drew:

Did you count the number of ones in the first drawing? It is not uncommon for students to make a total of ten instead of place an additional ten ones next to those they already have. Now they are ready to remove twenty-nine. Take a careful look at the drawing. It looks like ten have already been removed. For students who don't understand or remember all of the steps of the procedure their final drawing may be:

It looks like these students did remove twenty-nine but they didn't.

I understand why this correct drawing would be confusing to some students.

It looks like thirty-nine has been removed from seventy-two.

Think about what a student who has started with a vertical symbol-by-symbol drawing has to work out.

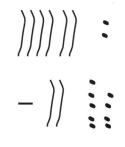

It isn't pretty.

As we're thinking about the materials students may use to solve problems, we need to be cognizant of our focus. Are we using the materials to build conceptual understandings or to model specific procedures? We also need to be mindful of the pictorial representations students draw. They tell us a great deal about their mathematics understandings. Do the pictures represent the models of the operations that we examined in Chapter 3?

To help students connect the various representations I have them organize their work into a four-part chart. For our subtraction problem we might see:

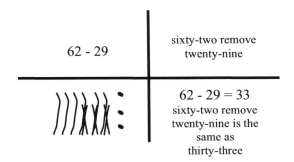

Students begin by recording the original expression 62 − 29. They then write the conceptual language translation. They draw a picture. In the last section they write the final equation in symbols and in words. Notice the use of number-words instead of symbols in the language translations. This provides students with practice writing number-words without doing number-word–specific lessons.

Recording in this way helps students connect pictorial, verbal, and symbolic representations for the problems they are solving. For our "struggling" students, we are increasing the possibility of giving them access to the mathematics through one of their strengths. It may be through the tactile manipulation of concrete materials, the pictorial representation, the conceptual language use, or the symbolic representations. At the same time we are helping them strengthen a weakness by having them represent the mathematics in a variety of ways.

The purposeful selection of materials and activity design can enhance the mathematical language used by students. Some materials, such as regular dominoes, have a single representation for each number, one to nine. Other materials, such as ten-frame dominoes, can have a variety of representations for the quantities. This variety of representations lends itself to both naming the quantity and defending a choice using language such as, "I know because . . . ." However, if we aren't careful, manipulative materials can be used to model specific procedures instead of building conceptual understandings. In planning future mathematical experiences I hope you'll consider:

◆   The purpose in choosing a given material;
◆   The ways in which students will connect concrete, pictorial, verbal, and symbolic representations; and
◆   The ways in which the cognitive demand of the experience can be increased for some while providing other students with the gift of time to make sense of the mathematics they are doing.

Questions for Reflection

1. Consider the ways in which you use manipulative materials to teach computation. Are you helping build conceptual understandings or modeling specific procedures?
2. How could you modify the use of materials to build conceptual understandings while connecting to symbolic representations?

References

Hess, K. K. (2006). *Cognitive complexity: Applying Webb DOK Levels to Bloom's Taxonomy.* Dover, NH: National Center for Assessment.

Wright, R. J, Martland, J., & Stafford, A. K. (2000). *Early Numeracy. Assessment for Teaching and Intervention.* London, Thousand Oaks, CA: SAGE Publications Inc.

6

Changing the Order for Introducing Mathematical Language

Experience Then Name

I have always been terrible at learning vocabulary. I remember vocabulary lessons as a student. We were given a list of words we were to look up in the dictionary, or perhaps the teacher would tell us the definition. We would have to write the definitions . . . sometimes several times. I may have remembered them for a vocabulary test but then they were forgotten.

Times have changed. There are many techniques for teaching vocabulary. But many still begin with the introduction of the new word or term. The teacher may explain the word's meaning. Students may write the meaning in their own words. They then may illustrate the word, use it in writing tasks, or compare and contrast with other words.

Experience First—A Look at Symmetry

This front loading of vocabulary has been a common technique used for teaching mathematical terminology. We introduce new terms to the students before they use them within the lesson. A definition or explanation of the term is given along with examples and perhaps counterexamples. This is how I learned about symmetry . . . and taught it for many years. I'd introduce the term "symmetry." I'd give several examples including butterflies, fish, and others from nature. I may remember to throw in a couple of non-examples and then the students practiced finding lines of symmetry and completing a design to make it symmetrical.

What if we change the sequence? What if we gave students an experience in which they worked with symmetry without even knowing it and then we named it? We know that spatial visualization is an important component of geometry as well as other areas of mathematics (Wheatley, 1997). Consider beginning a unit on symmetry with a visualization task (NCTM, 2000).

Materials: $5\frac{1}{2} \times 8\frac{1}{2}$ sheets of paper (half sheets of letter paper); scissors; projector

1. Fold the paper in half.
2. Make cuts to the paper.
3. Project the folded, cut paper and point to the fold line.

4. Tell students to draw what they think it will look like open.
5. Open the paper and allow students to "fix" their drawing if needed.
6. After completing three or four designs, have students discuss with a partner their strategies for drawing the opened design.
7. Invite students to share their partners' strategies for drawing the opened design.
8. Give students two or three additional folded designs to draw.

Notice that we have not introduced the term "symmetry" yet. I bet that as the designs get harder, your students will be drawing the fold line. Listening to and observing the strategies students use to draw the opened design is fascinating. Some students will draw exactly what they see and then "flip it over." That's a great transformational geometry term. The mathematical term is "reflect." When a student gives this explanation I typically ask, "So you drew what you saw and then you drew its reflection?" Hmmm! (I use Hmmm! a lot. It works for me. It means interesting!). Other students do a line-by-line reflection. They draw one line of what they see and then draw that line's reflection. I've had some students say they just picture what it looks like open and then draw it. The most fascinating to me is the technique of drawing a rectangle and then shading in what has been cut off. I just don't see things that way. Wow! It is also interesting to see which students change their technique after hearing the strategies their peers used.

At this point students have drawn what they think three or four folded and cut designs will look like opened. They have shared their strategies and tried to draw an additional two or three. Remember that how well they draw these designs, their accuracy, is not the goal of the lesson nor what I'm assessing. That's why we give them time to fix their drawings. What we're hoping for is that they draw that fold line. Don't require them to. Many of them will without prompting. That's the beauty of the activity. It provides an experience in which many of them will draw the line of symmetry before knowing its name. We just have to name it.

Let's return to the activity.

9. Display one or more of the opened designs and tell the students that you noticed that many of them drew the fold line. Invite them to compare their drawings with their neighbors' drawings.
10. Ask, "Does anyone know what that line is called?" If no one knows the term, introduce "line of symmetry."
11. Invite students to write an explanation of what they think a line of symmetry is. Encourage them to include drawings.

This single activity is not sufficient to build a depth of understanding about symmetry but it is a great start. It starts to build an understanding of a new mathematical term, line of symmetry.

Investigation to Try

Try the above activity with your students. Collect and review the students' explanations. What are their current understandings and what additional experiences are needed to refine their understandings?

One thing I've noticed when reading students' explanations is that they focus on the line cutting the shape in half. It does, but it does so in a special way. There is a difference between congruent halves and symmetrical halves. Consider the lines of symmetry for a square. There is a vertical line of symmetry,

a horizontal line of symmetry,

and two diagonal lines of symmetry.

Each of these halves are congruent and they are symmetrical. This is not the case for an oblong. Let's take a closer look. A non-square rectangle also has a vertical and horizontal line of symmetry.

 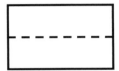

These are congruent and symmetrical halves. Is the diagonal line a line of symmetry?

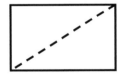

The diagonal cuts the oblong into congruent halves but it is not a line of symmetry. If you're not sure, test it. Fold a piece of paper along its diagonal. Do the two halves fold right on top of each other? They will only if the paper is that special, equilateral rectangle . . . a square. One of the great things about our introduction to symmetry was that we used this fold test for lines of symmetry. We began by showing half of a symmetrical shape.

Follow-up activities are needed and could include giving students shapes for which they find lines of symmetry. They can predict by drawing what they think will be lines of symmetry. They then cut out the shapes and fold along the lines to test if they are correct. Be sure to include a square and an oblong, as well as shapes with infinite lines of symmetry and no lines of symmetry (asymmetrical).

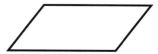

Invite students to revise their explanations of symmetry and lines of symmetry as they explore congruent halves, symmetrical halves, asymmetrical shapes, and shapes with infinite lines of symmetry. We hope that students' explanations become more precise as their understanding of symmetry grows. Don't forget about rotational symmetry. Give that a turn and then have them revise again.

Area Investigations

In Chapter 3 we examined a variety of models for multiplication. One of those models was the area model. A great introductory investigation is to have students find all of the rectangles that can be made with a given number of squares.

Materials:

Square tiles
Centimeter grid paper
1. Display four square tiles.

2. Ask, "What different rectangles could we make with these four squares?"
3. Have students discuss with a partner.
4. Invite students to share their conclusions.

They could be arranged four in a row horizontally,

four in a row vertically,

or as a two-by-two.

Don't be surprised if some students think that a square is not a rectangle. They may think that rectangles must be oblong. That tells you a bit about their previous experiences. Consequently, you will need to have a discussion about the characteristics of rectangles. We'll take a deeper look at this in Chapter 8.

As they share, have the students record the arrangements on the centimeter grid paper as shown. It is important that they outline the rectangles and write the number of squares used inside instead of coloring in the rectangles. Notice that I've left space between the rectangles and that I've included both the four by one and the one by four. Even though those rectangles are essentially the same, for our purposes it is important to show both orientations.

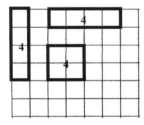

1. Ask students to find all of the rectangles that can be made using two squares, three squares, four squares, five, six, nine, and twelve squares. In each case they should record their findings on the grid paper and label with the number of squares that were used.

2. When complete the students should have something that looks like the graphic below.

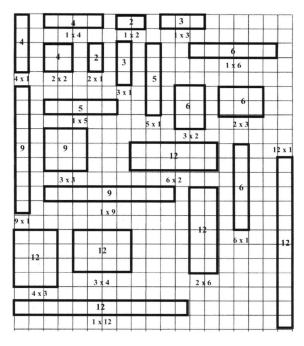

3. Underneath each rectangle, have the students record its dimensions.

4. Have students compare their drawings with a partner's. If they are missing any, they can add to their sheet. If they have duplicates, they can cross one of them out.

At this point, students have explored the area of rectangles, have hopefully verified or learned that squares are rectangles, and have described the dimensions of rectangles. These are all important pieces of the activity. But consider all of the mathematical terms that we can now introduce as a result of this experience.

By asking the students to show both orientations of the rectangles (e.g., 1×4 and 4×1) we can discuss the **Commutative Property**. The dimensions of the rectangles are the **factors**. We could list the factors for two of the numbers.

> **12:** 12, 6, 4, 3, 2, 1
> **9:** 9, 3, 1

We could then identify the **common factors** of three and one and the **greatest common factor**, three.

Because of including numbers such as four and nine, we can introduce the term **square numbers**. The area of a square is the square of its side length. That sounds confusing, but think about it. A square with side length of two has an area of four square units or two squared, 2^2. A square with side length of three has an area of nine square units or three squared, 3^2. What if we know the area of a square is nine square units? What is its side length? Three. What about a square with an area of sixteen square units? Four. So the **square root** of sixteen is four. The **square root** of nine is three. We have a geometric representation for the relationship of squares and square roots. Squaring involves knowing the side length and finding the area. Square roots involve knowing the area and finding the side length. At least this is true for whole numbers. We are beginning to build a conceptual understanding of these terms. As students are introduced to other number types, such as negative numbers and algebraic relationships, this understanding will expand. What would be the geometric relationship for cubes and cube roots? Hmmm!

Based on the investigation we introduced the following mathematical terms:

◆ Commutative Property
◆ Factors, common factors, greatest common factors
◆ Square numbers
◆ Square roots

We aren't done yet. Look at the numbers for which we could only draw two rectangles. For our investigation this includes two, three, and five. Those are **prime numbers**; exactly two rectangles, exactly two factors. The numbers for which we could draw more than two rectangles are **composite numbers**. I did not include the number one in our investigation. What about one? Is it prime or composite? Only one rectangle is possible. It will be a square with a side length of one. Therefore, one is a square number. But again, it only has one factor, 1. The definition I've heard for prime numbers is that it has itself and one as factors. It seems that one should be prime. However, this definition needs some refinement. A prime number has exactly two factors, one of which is one. The number one only has one factor. It is neither prime nor composite.

The challenge is, how do we continue to make this an investigation as we introduce terminology instead of turning it into a "lecture"? I could use think-pair-share to have the students tell me all they notice about the rectangles on their recording sheet. Someone typically mentions the squares. We can then introduce square numbers. For the Commutative Property I could display several sets of rectangle pairs from their work.

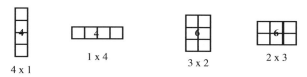

4 × 1   1 × 4   3 × 2   2 × 3

Using think-pair-share again, I could ask them what they notice about each of the pairs. One of the things they may notice is that whether it is a 4 × 1 or a 1 × 4 (when we turned it around) it still uses four squares. I could then ask if they know the name of the property. If not, I could introduce Commutative Property and then have them explain as we did with symmetry.

Questions for Reflection

1. What strategies could you use to introduce the other mathematical terms? What would the discussion sound like? What follow-up experiences would be needed?
2. Choose a mathematical term that students need to know at your grade level. What experience could you first provide and then name? What follow-up experiences would be needed to help students refine and deepen their understanding of the term?

Instead of front loading vocabulary, consider first giving students an experience. If carefully designed, these experiences provide a conceptual anchor to which students can connect new language. They are more memorable than what we may see when using a front-loading approach. Experience then name is a great technique for introducing terminology, but it is just the beginning. As we've discussed throughout the book, understanding and precisely using mathematical language takes time. Additional experiences will be needed to help students refine their understanding of the terms and related concepts. But what a great first step!

References

National Council of Teachers of Mathematics (2000). *Principles and Standards for School Mathematics*. Reston, VA: NCTM.

Wheatley, G. H. (1997). Reasoning with Images in Mathematical Activity. In L. D. English (Ed.), *Mathematical Reasoning. Analogies, Metaphors, and Images*. Mahwah, NJ: Lawrence Erlbaum Associates, Publishers.

7

Structuring Activities to Make Them Language Rich

Is it possible to be too helpful? Absolutely! Do we need to let students struggle with language and problem solving? Absolutely! Do we miss opportunities to have students use mathematical language? I think you know the answer . . . absolutely! Throughout the book we've investigated strategies for:

◆ Introducing terminology,
◆ Developing and using conceptual language,
◆ Connecting a variety of representations, and
◆ Expecting students to always defend their thinking.

We've also reminded ourselves of the importance of sitting down and being quiet. But is it possible to change a language-empty activity into a language-rich activity? Absolutely!

Have you or your students ever solved tangram puzzles? When I've observed students working on the puzzles they are typically alone. They may talk to others around them but they probably are not talking mathematics. However, with a few simple tweaks, this activity can be language rich.

Suppose that we made this a group activity? The group works together to solve the problem but only one child is allowed to touch the tangram pieces and puzzle sheet (Atkins, Bamberger, & Irons, 2001). However, that child cannot place a piece on the puzzle sheet without being told precisely where to place it. Suppose that each of the other children in the group took turns giving directions for tangram piece placement but could not point and could not say,

"Put it where it fits" or "Put it where it goes." A typical language-free individual activity now becomes language rich.

Tangram Communication Activity

Materials:

◆ Tangrams: One set for a group of three or four students
◆ Tangram puzzle sheets: Six to eight different puzzles, multiple copies of each puzzle (Copy each puzzle onto a different color of paper. It will assist in letting you know which groups have worked which puzzles.)

Players: Small groups of three or four

Roles

◆ **Tangram Robot:** A robot cannot do anything that it is not precisely told to do. It is very literal. One student will pretend he or she is a Tangram Robot. The Tangram Robot is the only one who can touch the pieces and the puzzle sheet. However, the Tangram Robot can only place the pieces where he or she is told in the exact way in which he or she is told. This player cannot "think" for herself. Even if she knows what the player meant to say or sees where the piece would fit, she must do *exactly* what she is told to do.
◆ **Tangram Puzzlers:** Remaining group members.

Directions:

1. Model the activity with the class. You take the role of the Tangram Robot and have students (Tangram Puzzlers) take turns telling you where to put the pieces. Model being very literal.

If a student says, "Put the triangle in the head." Pick up a triangle (especially one that is too big or too small) and set it down in the head. Don't be nice and put it where it obviously fits using the sized piece that you know works.

Make the students be precise in naming the size of the shape as well as tell you to turn it, slide it, or flip it over. If you don't, think of all of the language that is lost. [Remember our "experience then name" approach from Chapter 6. This is a great opportunity for students to naturally use the terms: flip, slide, and turn. After the activity we can introduce them to the mathematical terms: reflect, translate, and rotate.]

2. Have students select the starting Tangram Robot for their group of three or four.
3. Give a puzzle and a tangram set to the Tangram Robot.
4. Tangram Puzzlers take turns giving directions to the Tangram Robot.
5. When a group has completed a puzzle, have them select the next Tangram Robot and ask for a new puzzle sheet.
6. Continue until each student in the group has had at least one turn as the Tangram Robot.

Journal Prompt: Have the students leave the last completed puzzle displayed in the center of the group. Each student should write directions for completing the puzzle. Encourage students to be as detailed as possible.

You will have to keep an eagle eye on the players. Although they know they are not supposed to point, you'll see players jerk their head to one side or the other . . . pointing. This happens when adults play and it happens when children play. It is very hard to not point. Players will fold their hands to keep from pointing but keep an eye out for the pinky. The pinky will start moving as will one of the other fingers. If you look carefully the player is trying to show where they want the piece to go with that finger . . . pointing. They get very sneaky and very creative when you squelch the head jerking and folded-finger pointing. Watch them carefully!

Investigations to Try and Questions for Reflection

1. Try the Tangram Communication Activity with a group of three or four of your colleagues or friends. After each person has had a chance to be the Tangram Robot, work together to create a list of the math terms you used while doing the activity. Record in the left-hand column of a sheet of paper that you've folded in half vertically. Then think of the terms you would have used had you been able to point or say, "Put it where it fits." Record those terms in the right-hand column. Discuss how the use and quality of math terminology changed.
2. Complete the journal activity. Notice the language that was needed to write a solution description. How would the language experience change if students could draw the solution instead?

As you listen to your students or complete the above Investigation, consider the mathematical terms you are hearing. You will hear size terms such as small, medium, and large. You will hear shape names and attributes such as right angle and the long side. Players also use directional terms to specify the orientation of the shape. I've heard players use directions such as right and left but also north, south, east, west, and variations of those directions such as northwest. I've also heard students use the clock positions to describe orientations, three o'clock, six o'clock, etc. In Chapter 6 we examined strategies for providing experiences before introducing math terms. Through this experience students can be introduced to the terms **hypotenuse**, **obtuse**, **acute**, **right angles**, and **vertex**.

Players will also say things like, "Turn it until I say stop" or "Slide it until I say stop" or "flip it." These are terms associated with transformational geometry. They are also terms that disappear during the activity if the Tangram Robot is too nice and puts the piece where he or she thinks it is supposed to go. All of the language disappears if pointing is allowed. Creating language-rich activities requires the purposeful design of an activity and the purposeful use of materials.

Memory- or Concentration-Type Activities

I think memory- or concentration-type activities are great for helping students build connections. I admit the way I had students play these games wasn't very language rich. I doubt it helped them make connections either. The focus was on remembering where cards were located.

If you've ever played concentration or memory, you know that a set of cards is placed upside-down in an array so that it is a little easier to remember card location. Players take turns turning over two cards. If the cards match, they take them. If not, they turn them back over.

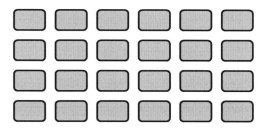

In watching students play this and other games I've noticed two types of players, hitchhikers and hit-and-run players. Hitchhikers wait for other players to tell them what they should do. In this game hit-and-run players take the two cards or turn the cards back over so quickly that the other players don't get to see the cards. There is very little mathematical language being used during the game. As we think of modifications to make this language-empty activity language rich and connection building, we also need to plan for these two types of players.

Materials: Card set for each group of three or four students

Directions:

1. Students mix the cards well before placing upside-down in a four by six array.
2. Players take turns trying to find matches.

   ◆ Player 1 turns two cards over and places them in their exact location. Player 1 then lifts his or her hands off of the cards. (No hit-and-run.)
   ◆ If the cards do not match, Player 1 must say why they do not match before turning the cards back over. If the cards do match, Player 1 must say why they do match before taking them. (No hitchhiking.)
   ◆ It's now Player 2's turn.

3. Play continues in this way until all of the cards have been paired.

Notice the ways in which we've increased the mathematical language used during the game. Students are using a great deal of mathematical language because they must always defend why the cards match or why they don't. Always defending also helps students build connections. Depending upon the card set, students may connect pictorial and symbolic representations, pictorial and verbal representations, or verbal and symbolic representations. It depends upon the ways in which you've designed the cards. I have sets that connect "6 + 6" to "double six" or a picture of half of a trapezoid to symbol ½.

Investigations to Try and Questions for Reflection

1. Use the cards provided in this book to play our memory matching game. Ensure each player defends whether he or she has a match or not. What mathematical language did you use while playing the game? What conceptual understandings were needed?
2. Design a card set appropriate for your students. You might choose a topic with which your students struggle. What don't they understand? What conceptual connections would you like them to make while playing the game?
3. Choose a mathematics activity that students typically complete independently. How could you redesign the activity to make it language rich without losing individual responsibility?

As you played the memory match game did you notice that one pair of cards did not match? When I've played these games I always figured that the leftover pair had to match. Consider what my level of thinking is at that point in the game. When I design the games, I sometimes have an uneven number of matches. Remember, even if they don't match, the player must defend why they don't. A great extension or journal prompt is for students to determine how one of the cards should be modified to make a match.

With a little strategic planning, language-empty activities can become language rich. Consider how domino activities developed mathematical language in Chapter 5. Solving tangram puzzles is no longer an independent activity. If we are purposeful in setting up the activity, it can become a group activity with wonderful opportunities to describe shape attributes, name shapes, and introduce transformational geometry terms. By adding a defense component, memory- or concentration-type games shift from remembering card location to using mathematical language to defend a match or non-match. We may want to sit down and be quiet but we want students to talk, talk, talk . . . and write about mathematics.

Reference

Atkins, S. L., Bamberger, H. J., & Irons, C. (2001). *Geometry & Spatial Problem Solving. Module 5.* Bothell, WA: INSIGHT.

8

Building Precision and Flexibility in Using Mathematical Language

Throughout the book I've mentioned moments that got my attention. Most involved learning about student understandings during class discussions or interviews. Reading the article, "Educating Hannah: It's a What?" provided another one of those attention-getting moments. In the article, Cockcroft and Marshall (1999) describe a conversation between two sisters.

> "Oh gosh!" said Hannah. "You've been completely misled if you think there are thick and thin plane shapes."

> (p. 327)

Hannah makes this comment after she and her sister discussed whether there was such a thing as a thick or thin circle. This article not only got my attention, it made my head hurt after reading and discussing. Wow!

I have a stack of construction paper circular discs that I cut using a die cut machine. They are all the same size. Suppose I were to hold up one of the discs and ask your students its name. What would they say? Circle? Let's say I stack five of those discs together. Would they still say circle? How about ten discs? How thick would the stack need to get before your students would change their answer to cylinder? The next question is, "At what point did it change from being a circle to becoming a cylinder? I ask this question when working with teachers and students. Both groups answer, "When it has thickness."

How can something get thicker if it didn't have thickness in the first place? That was the point Hannah was making. Two-dimensional shapes do not have a thickness, three-dimensional shapes do. As I said, that started me thinking. My paper discs were really cylinders . . . even when it was a single disc.

Have you ever used pattern blocks during lessons? I have. What did you call the yellow shape? Hexagon? How about the green shape? Triangle? Were they a quarter-inch thick or the thinner ones? Hmmm! How about attribute blocks? Do you have the sets with thin and thick circles or thin and thick rectangles? Think of Hannah's point. Thickness is not an attribute of two-dimensional shape. If I'm precise, I should not use terms of thickness with two-dimensional shape names. I think you could have a thin or thick cylinder but not a circle. The shapes in those sets are cylinders and prisms.

Attention to precision, especially in our use of mathematical language, is an important aspect of developing conceptual understanding (Oberdorf & Taylor-Cox, 1999). If we aren't careful, students can develop misconceptions, such as 2D shapes are thick or thin, instead of the desired conceptual understandings. When interviewing students, I'm no longer surprised by those students who think a square is not a rectangle. If we don't know they have this misconception in the early grades, we learn of it as students progress in mathematics. A common problem given in the upper grades asks students for the maximum rectangular area that can be enclosed with a given amount of fencing. It will be a square. But what if the student thinks a square is not a rectangle? Not good.

I began the book by discussing strategies for finding out what kids really think. As I've said, many kids think a square is not a rectangle. We don't want our investigation to end with what they think. The next question we need to ask ourselves is, "Why would they think that? What experiences have they had that would lead them to that conclusion?"

Traditionally, children are first introduced to circles, triangles, and squares. They then learn about a new shape, the rectangle. It is described as having two long sides and two shorter sides. It makes sense that students would think they were different shapes. Wouldn't it be preferable to prevent this misconception if possible? There is a relatively simple fix. What if we first introduce children to circle, triangle, and rectangle. We then introduce the square as a special rectangle. It's the one with equal sides. This one simple switch in order helps build the needed conceptual understandings.

Questions for Reflection

What are the minimum requirements for a shape to be a rectangle? Do we need to say it has four right angles or is three sufficient? Could you draw a four-sided closed shape with three right angles that is not a rectangle? How about two right angles? If you can, how would I need to revise my question so that you can only draw a rectangle? What if we first say it's a parallelogram? Would saying it has two right angles then be sufficient? Could you draw a parallelogram with two right angles that is not a rectangle?

There is a lot to think about with something as "simple" as a rectangle. It's not as simple as we might have thought. After reading the above discussion, where do you think three-dimensional shapes fit in? Our world is made up of 3D shapes. We can touch them. I won't suggest that we should perhaps start with 3D shapes instead of 2D in this chapter. But I'm sure you could predict what I'd say. Read the article. I will say that a cube is a special rectangular prism. It is the one with congruent faces. Hmmm!

In a language-rich mathematics class, students are given many opportunities to describe and defend their thinking. They connect a variety of representations including concrete, pictorial, verbal, and symbolic. Language-rich mathematics classes also require students to listen to and value what their peers have to say.

One of my favorite activities for building connections and getting students to listen carefully is "I Have . . . Who Has?" If you aren't familiar with this activity, each student is given a card (be sure to mix well first). On the top half of the card is a statement that begins, "I have . . . ." The bottom half of the card contains the question, "Who has . . . ?" The statements and questions may be followed by words or by pictures that the student must interpret (e.g., pictures of a collection of coins of which the student must determine the total value).

Play begins with the first person reading the question half of his card. Whoever has the answer reads the top half of her card beginning with "I have . . . ." She then reads the question at the bottom of her card. If all goes well, everyone will have a chance to read the statement and question on their card and it will end with the starting person reading the "I have . . ." portion of his card. One thing I forgot to mention . . . after distributing the cards, give your students time to determine what their card "says" before launching into the activity. It is important that they first have think time before listening to the questions.

Let's look at some sample cards from the set included in this book.

I have pi. **Who has** an equilateral rectangle?	**I have** a square. **Who has** an equilateral quadrilateral?	**I have** a rhombus. **Who has** a triangle with unequal sides?

Notice that we want to be flexible in our use of terms and include more than shape names. We want to include the characteristics of shape or other terms that can be used to describe shapes and build conceptual understandings (e.g., equilateral rectangle).

In the sample set provided, I've focused on measurement and shape. I could also design cards that build fluency with conceptual language translations. For example,

I have **Who has** four groups of four?	**I have** sixteen. **Who has** double eight and one more?	**I have** $8 + 9$. **Who has** twenty-four separated into two equal groups?
I have a dozen. **Who has** three fewer than forty?	**I have** $40 - 3$. **Who has** ???	

Are there any that were particularly challenging, made you stop and think, or were a surprise? As I write these they are in order, but remember we mix them well before we distribute to the students.

Investigations to Try and Questions for Reflection

1. Complete the set of cards that I began above or choose a topic and design your own set of cards. Try the cards with your class. Which cards did they find challenging? It's more than a game. It is a great assessment tool.
2. Have your students create their own set of "I Have . . . Who Has . . . ?" cards. Again, this is a great assessment of their current understandings. What did you learn from them?

To me, geometric terminology is loaded. The name of a shape carries with it a set of characteristics that give the shape that classification. I know this is true for all language. Geometry seems different for some reason. In Chapter 6 I used terms such as non-square rectangle, equilateral rectangle, oblong. It may have seemed over the top at the time. But as we've seen, our language can build conceptual understandings as well as misconceptions. If we want to ensure students understand squares are also rectangles, in what other ways can we name the shape? Equilateral rectangle? How would we describe rectangles that aren't squares? Oblong? Non-square rectangle?

The goal is for students to hear and use precise terminology. However, we don't want this precision to get in the way of students discussing their mathematical ideas. Precise does not mean rigid. We want to keep in mind that there are many mathematically correct ways to describe and defend solutions.

You may have guessed that I have a passion for working with struggling students in mathematics. I firmly believe the first step to intervention is prevention. I think it is easier to try to prevent a misconception than to fix it later. I don't want to give an attribute of thickness to a 2D shape. That said, I am as precise as possible in my use of language.

As we've seen, conceptual understanding involves much more than symbol naming and shape identification. It involves understanding the models and characteristics the symbols represent. It also involves a precision in the use of mathematical terms and language. We've repeatedly examined the importance of students being flexible in the ways they describe and represent key mathematical concepts and terms. We've also investigated techniques for introducing, refining, and expanding a student's understanding of a concept and its related language (precision). This flexibility and precision enables students to approach problems, especially non-routine problems, from a variety of angles.

Questions for Reflection

1. How would inattention to precision affect a student's conceptual understandings?
2. Are there examples from your own practice in which a lack of precision or inflexibility in the students' previous experiences affected their ability to solve mathematics problems? What experiences are needed to help students rethink, refine, or expand their understandings?

References

Cockcroft, W. H. & Marshall, J. (1999). Educating Hannah: It's a What? *Teaching Children Mathematics, 5*(6), 326–329.

Oberdorf, C. D & Taylor-Cox, J. (1999). Shape Up! *Teaching Children Mathematics, 5*(6), 340–345.

9

Making Sense of Word Problems
Developing Independent
Problem Solvers

All students seem to struggle with word problems. Their struggle is often a language struggle. It reflects our primary use of symbolic decoding language (plus, minus, times, divided by) during the majority of our mathematical work. We save "word problem" language for word-problem–specific lessons. Consequently, when they read word problems students struggle with choosing the appropriate operation. In the previous chapters we've examined strategies for developing the language of word problems in all we do. In this chapter let's delve deeper into techniques that have been used in the past and recommendations for building independence in solving word problems.

Beware of Key Words

A popular technique for helping students with word problems is key words. Students are taught the words that typically represent each operation. In many cases these key word lists become very extensive. In searching key word charts I've found the following words listed just for addition.

add
plus
sum
total
added to

more
both
in all
more than
join
raise
gain of
additional
together
put together
combined
increase
increased by
altogether

Instead of reading to understand the problem, I've observed many students scanning a problem for these key words. They then use the related operation on the numbers and hope they get the correct answer.

We can write word problems to assess if students are relying on a key word approach. Suppose I give students the following problem:

> Max collects signed baseballs. He had 23 baseballs. He got some more for his birthday. He now has 28 in all. How many baseballs did he get for his birthday?

If they use a key word approach, they may think that they are to add the two quantities together because of the terms "in all" and "more." But this is a problem in which the change is unknown. We are trying to find how many more. This can be represented as a missing addend or a subtraction problem. Students who are relying on key words without understanding the problem may say that the answer is fifty-one. It is important that students know the meaning of the operations and the language used, as well as understand the problem before solving.

Building Independent Problem Solvers

How many times have you distributed papers to your students when several hands shot up before the paper settled on the desk? It seems to be a cause-and-effect relationship. Math sheet goes out . . . hands go up requesting help. I wish this would happen after students at least look at the printed side or, better yet, read what was asked. We've all had students who are very dependent on receiving assistance in math. When it comes to word problems I found that I inadvertently encourage this dependence on me.

In the past, if you visited my class for a word problem lesson, you might see the following:

- ◆ Someone reads the problem aloud to the class. I may read it, a student may read it, or the class reads it together.
- ◆ I would guide the students in highlighting or underlining the important information.
- ◆ We'd then discuss how we could solve the problem. I might have students talk me through the solution, but I would do the writing.
- ◆ We would repeat this process for two or three problems. Then students would have time for independent practice. The practice problems would be very similar to the sample problems.

I hate to admit it but I tried to use this procedural approach to solving word problems. I tried to remove the problem solving from solving word problems. I had students focused on getting the answer before helping them learn to understand the problem.

I used this approach for the months prior to the high-stakes tests. When testing week arrived I essentially pulled the rug out from under them. We couldn't read as a class. We couldn't highlight important information together. We couldn't solve as a group. We had practiced reading and solving problems as a group and now they couldn't have assistance.

This attention-getting moment came in watching fifth-graders try to solve two pretty simple problems. They actually had three problems that they were solving. It was watching what they did with Problems 2 and 3 that got my attention. Problem 2 was:

Daniel is stocking shelves at a local grocery store. He has 98 cans that he is putting in rows of 10. How many rows will he have?

The students had highlighted "98 cans," "rows of 10," and "How many rows." Problem 3 was:

Suppose that in Problem 2, Daniel put the cans in rows of 13. How many rows will he have?

What do you think the students highlighted? You're correct if you thought "rows of 13," "How many rows," and "Problem 2."

I wasn't surprised the students had highlighted those particular pieces of information. I was surprised when I asked a student what was happening in Problem 3 and she pointed to an equation on her paper, "2 × 13 = 26." Where did the "2" come from? Well it did state that "in Problem 2 . . . ." I'd like to say that she was the only one. Unfortunately I can't. I asked again, "What is going on in this problem? What is this a problem about?" After a long pause she said, "Cans? On shelves?" This was not an obscure context. If students have been in a grocery store, they have seen rows of cans on shelves. But they had somehow missed that the problem scenario should first make sense before trying to solve the problem. If she understood the problem, the mathematics needed to solve it would make sense.

Problem Solving Graphic Organizer

I now use a four-part graphic organizer to build independence and to help students make sense of problems.

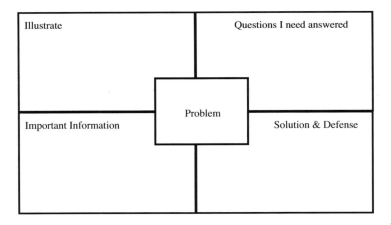

Illustrate: After reading the problem independently, each student draws a picture to represent the problem. It is important for students to realize that mathematical illustrations do not need to be elaborate. Stick people don't need fancy outfits or accessories. They might not be needed at all. In mathematics an "*x*" or "*o*" may be used to represent people. I purposely begin with problems for which illustrations can be simple and would make sense. Eventually I add problems in which the "illustration" may be a chart or some other diagram.

Questions I need answered: If students have questions about the problem, they write those questions in the "Questions I need answered" section. This is a space for each student to write any questions that he or she needs answered to help him or her understand the problem. Students may ask questions about what a word or abbreviation means. They may ask for clarification about the problem. If a student has no questions, this section would be blank. It will more than likely be different for each student. What this is *not*:

- ◆ A space to ask how to solve the problem.
- ◆ A space for rewriting the question to be answered in the problem.
- ◆ A space that looks the same for all students.

If a student has a question, he lets his partner know. The partner reads the question and tries to answer it. If she has the same question or doesn't know the answer, the students ask another pair at their table group. If no one knows the answer, the students let me know. I stop the class and have the students ask their questions of the class. If no one knows, we discuss where we could find the answer. Students may say the textbook, a dictionary, the Internet. One of the hardest changes for me was to remember that I am not the answer key (see Chapter 4). As the answer key, I was not modeling problem solving and I lost these valuable research opportunities.

Important Information: In this section students write what is important to remember. For example, "I need to give two answers" or "They give the dimensions in yards and they want the answer in feet." Students may draw an arrow from their illustration into the box because the drawing contains all of the important information. Students can also compute in this box.

Solution and Defense: In this last section, the students both state the answer and defend their answer in words. The leading sentence would be as simple as, "The answer is _____ because . . . ." The written form is persuasive writing (proof) instead of process writing. They are not describing how they solved the problem. They are trying to convince their peers that their answer is correct.

The Word Problem Solving Process

Initially, a word problem is placed in the center of the chart. Students read the problem independently. They then complete the sections of the chart independently. If they have questions they need answered, they first consult with a peer, then their table group. If they are unable to get the needed answers, we discuss as a class. When they complete the problem they begin the next problem. I have four or five problems available, each getting progressively harder. I also have some "simpler" word problems available for students who may initially struggle with the process or the math focus. In this way I'm able to differentiate the experience. As students become comfortable with the process they can either fold a sheet of paper into four sections or draw the chart in their journals. Eventually they will include these sections without needing to organize into a four-part chart.

Sample Problem 1—Introducing the Process: Below is the first problem I give students to introduce them to this process. The problem is simple and it is pretty easy for students to draw a picture of the jumping contest.

1. Each student receives a copy of the problem sheet.
2. Ask the students to read the problem silently. In the top left-hand box they are to draw a picture to represent the problem. If they have any questions, they are to write those in the top right-hand box. The rules are:

   ◆ We are doing math sketches, not elaborate illustrations.
   ◆ You may not ask how to solve the problem.
   ◆ You may ask questions to help you understand the problem.
   ◆ If you have written a question, quietly let your partner know. When your partner is at a good stopping place, have him or her read and try to answer your question. If your partner does not know the answer, quietly ask the others in your table group. If no one knows, let me know by raising your hand.

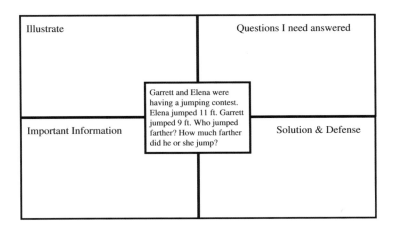

3. While students are working, travel the room to observe what they write. If you notice a student has written a question, ask if he has discussed it with his partner or the other members of his table group. I expected students to ask what "ft." or "yd." means; however, I was surprised when one student wrote, "Why didn't Garrett jump farther?" What can you say? Some questions don't really need answers.

4. After the majority of students have written something in one or both sections, interrupt the class. Ask if there are any questions that still need answers. As students ask their remaining questions, invite other students in the class to answer the questions. If no one knows the answer, ask the class how they could find those answers. Students may say look in the text, look in a dictionary, Google it, ask you. Don't give in to the "ask you" option. It is important for students to learn how to find answers to questions. Give students time to find the answers.

5. Remind students of the rules. You may find that further discussion is needed as to the characteristics of a math sketch.

6. Point to the "Important Information" box. Tell students that in this section they are to write information they need to remember when solving the problem. Give students time to record information they find important and then discuss as a class. This does not need to be a restating of the questions. For this problem it may be, "I need to answer two questions." Tell students they can also compute in this section.

7. Give students time to solve the problem. As a class, look at the final section of the chart, "Solution and Defense." Tell students that in this section they are to write the answer or answers to the questions and use words to convince everyone that the answer or answers are correct.

   Note: Remember that we are introducing students to the sections of the chart and the process they will use to complete the problems. At this point we have not examined student drawings or discussed the answer to the questions.

8. After students have completed their solution defenses, debrief as a class. Begin by having students fold their paper vertically

and horizontally so only the illustration is showing. Select the papers of three or four students who have different illustrations for the problem. Using a document camera, if available, display the four illustrations. Ask:

- Is it okay to have different illustrations for this problem?
- Does each drawing match the problem? If a student has a concern or disagrees, invite her to ask a question to help the owner change his or her mind.
- Do you have any tips or suggestions for improving the math sketch?

9. Give students a second problem. Have them work through the process independently. Use the same process as described above to handle student questions. At this point there is no need for students to work at the same pace. Have two or three additional problems available. The problems in the set should get increasingly more difficult. After students complete the solution defense (in words) of a problem, they get the next problem in the sequence. The goal is for all of the students in the class to complete the first two or three problems and for some students to be challenged with the additional problems.

Sample Problem 2—Debriefing Problems: One of the key mathematical practices is constructing viable arguments and critiquing the reasoning of others (National Governors Association Center for Best Practices & Council of Chief State School Officers, 2010). Unfortunately, we lose opportunities for students to engage in this practice by helping them find straight paths to solving word problems. That is, when we see them go astray we intervene a bit too soon. By doing so, we see very little variation in the solution methods and answers. Consequently, there is little to critique or defend. When giving students problems, allow them to go astray, be purposeful in any intervention you do take, and be patient. Finding those errors or missteps is what critiquing the reasoning of others is all about.

I gave the following problem to a group of fifth-graders. It was a great problem for me to learn about the students' misunderstandings. I hope it also provides examples of effective strategies for debriefing word problems.

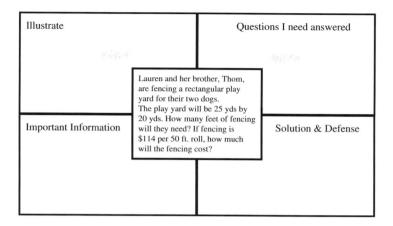

Illustrate	Questions I need answered

Lauren and her brother, Thom, are fencing a rectangular play yard for their two dogs. The play yard will be 25 yds by 20 yds. How many feet of fencing will they need? If fencing is $114 per 50 ft. roll, how much will the fencing cost?

Important Information	Solution & Defense

The students had no problem drawing a picture of a rectangular play yard with dimensions 20 × 25 yards. Some students wrote questions such as, "What does yds stand for?" or "How many feet in a yard?" Later they asked if you had to buy a whole roll of fencing. Under "Important Information" some had written "gives lengths in yards wants answer in feet" and "needs two answers." They worked through the process beautifully. But as I walked around the room looking at their solutions, I repeatedly saw an answer of 500. I was wondering how in the world they got 500. Then it hit me. They were finding the area and not the perimeter. One student, Dante, even drew a picture with the fencing on the inside.

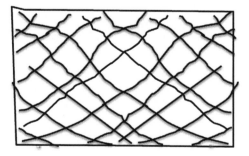

It was so tempting to ask, "Is this a problem about area or perimeter?" or say, "Now remember, you're finding the perimeter, not the area." But what would have happened had I done so? I would have lost the opportunity for the students to defend and critique. That said, I did feel like I needed to throw a wrench in the students' thinking.

I interrupted the class and asked them what answers they had for the amount of fencing they needed. The students said, "500," "1,500," "4,500," and "2,025." Some students were still working on the problem. I began by asking if this is the type of problem that has multiple correct answers. I gave the students time to discuss with their partners. We then discussed as a class. They decided that there should be just one answer. I then asked the students to describe what was being asked in the problem. They knew that they were to find the amount of fencing. I had Dante display his drawing and asked where the fencing was going. He pointed to the interior of the rectangle. Several of the students looked puzzled. Instead of telling Dante where the fence should go, the students were used to asking questions to help their peers change their minds. Chantel asked, "Are they walking on the fence?" Dante then looked puzzled. I asked Chantel to show where the fence should go. She outlined the perimeter of the rectangle. That was all that was needed. The students were quickly back to work revising their solutions. The first thing Dante did was to change his drawing. He erased the fence on the inside. The illustration needed to match his understanding of the problem.

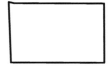

Don't think that everything went smoothly after that. The students did get back to work and they did find the perimeter instead of the area. However, when I asked how much fencing was needed I heard forty-five, ninety, 135, 180, 270, and 500. We again discussed if this question would have multiple correct answers or just one. Again, the students decided it should have one correct answer for the perimeter. I asked, "Which of these don't work and why?" One student said forty-five because it's too low. I then asked, "If someone got forty-five as an answer, what do you think they didn't understand or what mistake did they make?" This is a great way to have students critique the reasoning of others. This is also a great way to assess the students' understanding of the problem.

In this same fifth-grade class there was a student, Precious, who did a fantastic job of describing why 135 was incorrect. She was actually the only one in the class who had raised her hand with an idea. Great! Someone else had said that 180 was incorrect and had described why it didn't work. At that point we were left with 270 and a student was about to defend that answer. Then Precious interrupted. She said that she still thought that 180 was a correct answer. It was fantastic that Precious felt comfortable interrupting and defending an answer that others had removed. When I asked her why she thought that 180 was correct, she said, "You have twenty-five twice and twenty twice. That's ninety. There are two dogs so that's 180." Wow!

I would have missed Precious' using the number of dogs had I intervened too soon or had we gone straight to identifying and defending the correct answer. How often do we assume that students understand the solution to the problem because we "went over it"? In this case, I didn't realize that extraneous information was an issue for some students. Precious opened that door and we were able to then discuss as a class. Thank you, Precious!

Instructional Guidelines

1. Don't intervene too soon. Allow students to have missteps. Handle those during the class debriefing.
2. Gather all of the answers students have for the problems.
3. Launch with, "Is this the type of problem that has multiple correct solutions?"
4. Ask, "Are there any answers that you think don't work? Why not?," or if a student disagrees, invite them to ask a question to help their peers change their minds.
5. Don't let debriefing become, "Now I'll show you how I thought about it or," "Here's how you could have solved it."

Sample Problem 3—Don't Let Your Past Interfere With the Students' Problem Solving: Many of us were taught very procedural approaches to solving mathematics problems. For those of us who have taught for any length of time, we've also taught very procedural answer-getting techniques to our students (Daro, 2014). Remember, those answer-getting approaches aren't always the easiest way to think about a problem. Consider the following problem.

Collin and Chloe are having a party on the 25th. Seventy-five people were invited. They will have cake, chips, and soda. How many two-liter bottles of soda will they need to buy if each person gets 250 ml of soda?

We would begin by finding the total number of milliliters that are needed for the seventy-five people attending.

$$
\begin{array}{r}
250 \\
\times\,75 \\
\hline
1250 \\
17500 \\
\hline
18750
\end{array}
$$

We know that we need 18,750 ml for the party. We'd then try to remember which way to move the decimal point and how many places we needed to move it. We might even know a mnemonic to help us with this. In the end we hope that 18,750 ml is equivalent to 18.75 liters. Rereading the problem we'd see that we are to find the number of 2-liter bottles. Assuming we can't buy partial bottles we will need ten 2-liter bottles. This approach requires proficiency with multi-digit multiplication and recalling the procedure for converting milliliters to liters or at least remembering the mnemonic for ordering the metric prefixes so that we can move the decimal point. It was the way many of us were taught to solve this type of problem. But it is not the only way.

This problem can also be viewed as a ratio problem. If each person gets 250 milliliters, then two people get 500 ml.

One person: 250 ml
Two people: 500 ml

Double again and four people get 1,000 ml or a liter.

Four people: 1,000 ml or 1 liter

If we double again we'd find that two liters are needed for every eight people.

Eight people: 2 liters

Nine sets of eight would equal seventy-two, but there are seventy-five people at the party so we will need ten 2-liter bottles. Solving the problem in this way relies less on recalling facts and procedures and more on reasoning about the relationships described in the problem. Although this second approach involves algebraic reasoning, I find it much easier. What do you think?

The key to helping students make sense of problems and persevere in solving them is to develop the language of mathematics in all that we do.

Fluency with the conceptual language associated with the operations allows students to identify the needed operation but more importantly to reason about the relationships in problems, defend their reasoning and resulting solutions, and critique the reasoning of others. Each of these requires precise use and understanding of mathematical language.

Investigations to Try and Questions for Reflection

Select four or five word problems to try this approach with your students. These may come from math resources that you have available or you may choose to write your own. Be sure that each new problem is more challenging than the previous. Also have some simpler word problems available for students who may initially struggle with this process.

1. What questions did students need answered so that they could understand the problem? Were their group mates able to answer or did it become a whole-class investigation? What follow-up activities are needed to either fill a mathematics concept gap or extend students' understanding of the concepts?
2. Ask your students to write story problems for use with your class. I often do this after completing an investigation. I say, "Suppose you were writing the math book. What questions would you ask students to solve?" Review the problems your students wrote. What did you learn about their understandings?

References

Daro, P. (2014, August 1). *Phil Daro Against Answer Getting SD* (YouTube Video). Retrieved from https://www.youtube.com/watch?v=DgTnmRyV9bc

National Governors Association Center for Best Practices & Council of Chief State School Officers. (2010). *Common Core State Standards for Mathematics.* Washington, DC: Authors.

Conclusion
Give Students the Gift of Time

I met Connor in May of his first-grade year. Connor was one of four children in an intervention group. At first sight Connor just seemed to be going through the motions. He appeared to know that you move objects when counting but didn't appear to actually count the objects. He knew that when you counted using the hundreds chart you point to numbers on the chart. He pointed but he didn't point to the same numbers that were being said aloud. When asked to locate a number given verbally he couldn't. At first sight Connor seemed to need a lot of support.

My conversation with Connor was another attention-getting moment for me. The next day I did some quick image activities with Connor to determine if he could subitize quantities to five and ten. Connor had a whiteboard and a marker to record his answers. I had a variety of cards with different number representations: symbols, domino dot images, and five-frame images.

I quickly showed,

I asked Connor to write how many he saw. He wrote "7."
I quickly showed,

I again asked Connor, "how many?" He said and wrote "4."
I then showed,

This time I asked, "How many more to make five?" Connor said, "two."
I asked him to write it down. He started to draw. It took a little while but he
drew,

He paused and seemed to be thinking so I waited. He look at me to see
my reaction and I just smiled and waited. He then finished his drawing.

My first reaction upon seeing the completed five-frame was to assist
Connor. After all, he seemed to be struggling and his drawing wasn't
quite what I had expected or hoped for. But by waiting, by giving him the
gift of time, I learned how much Connor did know. He was able to show
and defend his thinking. I was underestimating Connor. That got my
attention!

We asked another first-grader, Shannon, to join us. I showed Shannon,

I asked her how many and she said "five." I showed it to her again and
she still said "five." I set it down on the table, five. I asked Connor how many.
He said "six." I asked Shannon again and she said "five." I asked Connor if
he thought it was six, could he explain it to Shannon to help her change her
mind? He took the card. He turned it.

He covered the single dot with his finger and said as he pointed to the filled five-frame, "This is five." He uncovered the dot and said, "This is six." He spun the card different ways showing it was five with the dot covered and six with the dot uncovered. He explained his thinking and did a wonderful job of defending why the total was six instead of five. I had definitely underestimated Connor's ability to participate in a language-rich conversation.

As time passed, Connor became more confident, more animated. He was showing understanding, not going through the motions of doing what he was asked to do but not understanding why. All students, including Connor, need the gift of time to think, to build connections between a variety of representations, to determine what they want to say, and to build confidence in their ability to discuss mathematical ideas. They also need to feel safe to have missteps in their use of language.

Throughout the book we've examined techniques for building conceptual understanding and creating a language-rich mathematics class. As we've discussed, it takes time to develop mathematical language. It requires us to sit down, be quiet, be curious, and listen to what the children are saying. With children like Connor, that gift of time, extra time, is critical. Without it, his understanding and ability to engage in a language-rich conversation is overlooked or perhaps squelched.

Now that our time is coming to an end, I'll close with one last story. I recently observed some students exploring fractional relationships. In particular, they were discussing how pieces get smaller as the denominators get larger. They were repeatedly folding a piece of fabric. After each fold, they named the piece and talked about its size in relation to the whole. They had folded it in half, fourths, eighths, and sixteenths. The student helper was trying to fold it one more time. He did. The teacher again asked what they should call the new unit. Several students said, "thirty-seconds (32nds)." Then I heard one student say, "Can also mean thirty seconds on the clock." Don't you just love that?

Questions for Reflection

1. Did you have any AHA moments while reading this book? What were they?
2. Which strategies have you tried with your students that led to language-rich moments?
3. Which strategies do you think will help students who are struggling in mathematics have AHA moments?

Blackline Masters

Ten-Frame Dominos

Sample Concentration Game Cards

500	750
875	625
50	150
200	300

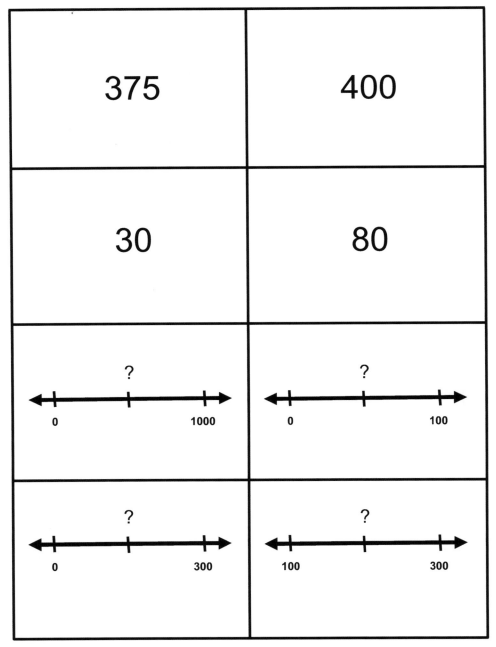

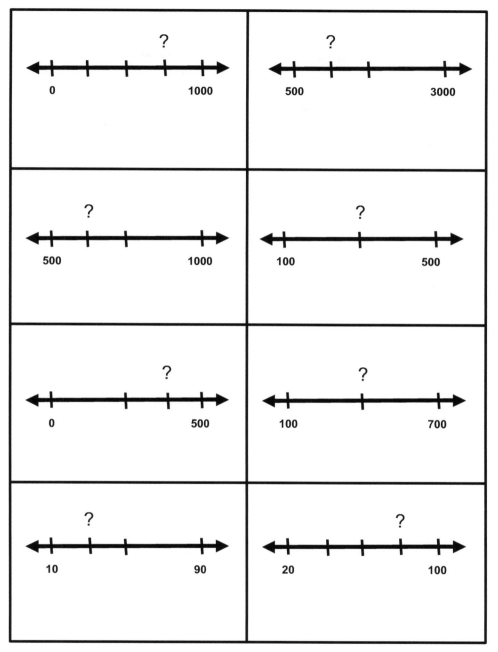

Tangram Piece Master

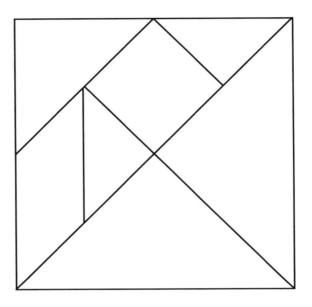

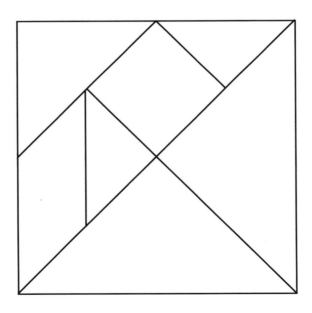

Sample Tangram Puzzles

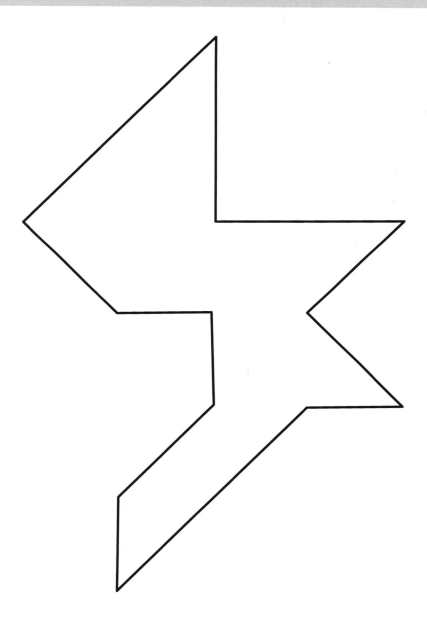

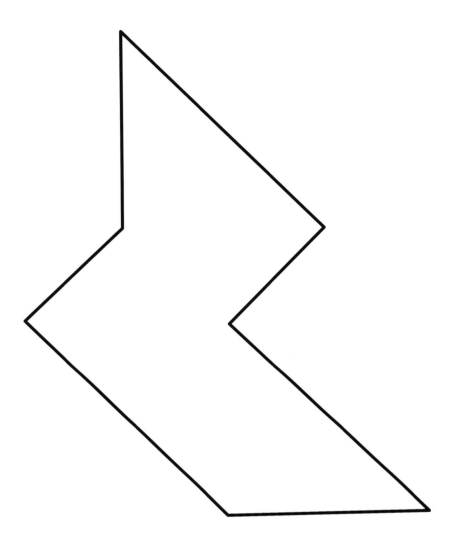

Sample "I Have . . . Who Has?" Cards

I have pi. **Who has** an equilateral rectangle?	**I have** a square. **Who has** an equilateral quadrilateral?
I have a rhombus. **Who has** a triangle with unequal sides?	**I have** a scalene triangle. **Who has** an equilateral 6-sided shape?
I have a regular hexagon. **Who has** a quadrilateral with only one set of parallel sides?	**I have** a trapezoid. **Who has** a 3D box shape?
I have a rectangular prism. **Who has** an angle less than 90 degrees?	**I have** an acute angle. **Who has** the sum of the angle measures in a triangle?

I have 180 degrees. Who has a regular rectangular prism?	I have a cube. Who has an angle more than 90 degrees?
I have an obtuse angle. Who has a ten-sided shape?	I have a decagon. Who has the degree measure of a right angle?
I have 90 degrees. Who has the tool used to measure angles?	I have a protractor. Who has a can shape?
I have a cylinder. Who has a triangle with two equal sides?	I have an isosceles triangle. Who has a shape with 2 triangular and 3 rectangular faces?

I have a triangular prism. **Who has** the segment from the circle's center to its edge?	**I have** a radius. **Who has** the segment that is twice my length?
I have a diameter. **Who has** a five-sided shape?	**I have** a pentagon. **Who has** a twelve-faced polyhedron?
I have a dodecahedron. **Who has** a ten-faced polyhedron?	**I have** a decahedron. **Who has** the linear measure around a closed 2D shape?
I have perimeter. **Who has** the square measure of the space inside a closed shape?	**I have** area. **Who has** the ratio of circumference to diameter?

Word Problem Graphic Organizer

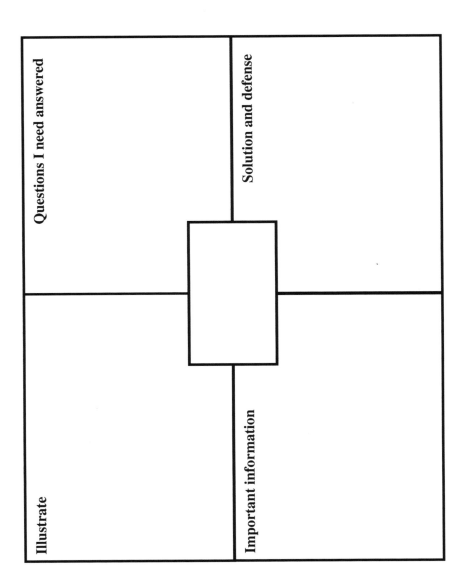

Illustrate

Questions I need answered

Important information

Solution and defense

Sample Word Problems

Illustrate

Questions I need answered

Garrett and Elena were having a jumping contest. Elena jumped 11 ft. Garrett jumped 9 ft. Who jumped farther? How much farther did he or she jump?

Important information

Solution and defense

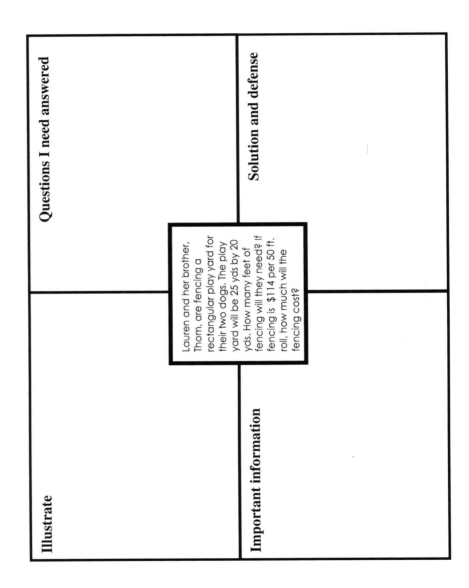

Questions I need answered

Solution and defense

Illustrate

Important information

Lauren and her brother, Thom, are fencing a rectangular play yard for their two dogs. The play yard will be 25 yds by 20 yds. How many feet of fencing will they need? If fencing is $114 per 50 ft. roll, how much will the fencing cost?

Questions I need answered	Illustrate
Collin and Chloe are having a party on the 25th. Seventy-five people were invited. They will have cake, chips, and soda. How many two-liter bottles of soda will they need to buy if each person gets 250 ml of soda?	
Solution and defense	Important information